Read 4 Today

Grade 4

Frank Schaffer Publications®

Editor: Linda Triemstra
Interior Designer: Lori Kibbey

Frank Schaffer Publications®

Send all inquiries to:
Frank Schaffer Publications
3195 Wilson Drive NW
Grand Rapids, Michigan 49534

Read 4 Today—grade 4

ISBN: 0-7682-3214-7

3 4 5 6 7 8 9 10 PAT 10 09 08 07

Read 4 Today

Table of Contents

Introduction

Read 4 Today supplies predictable, patterned review and practice materials for students. Four questions a day for four days a week provide students with the opportunity to hone their skills. A separate assessment is included for the fifth day of each week. On odd-numbered weeks, students will work on decoding or word strategies, vocabulary, fluency, and comprehension; on even-numbered weeks, the activities focus on book titles and previewing, with students answering questions before, during, and after reading. This book covers a forty-week period, and each grade level includes some curricula from the previous and the following grade levels.

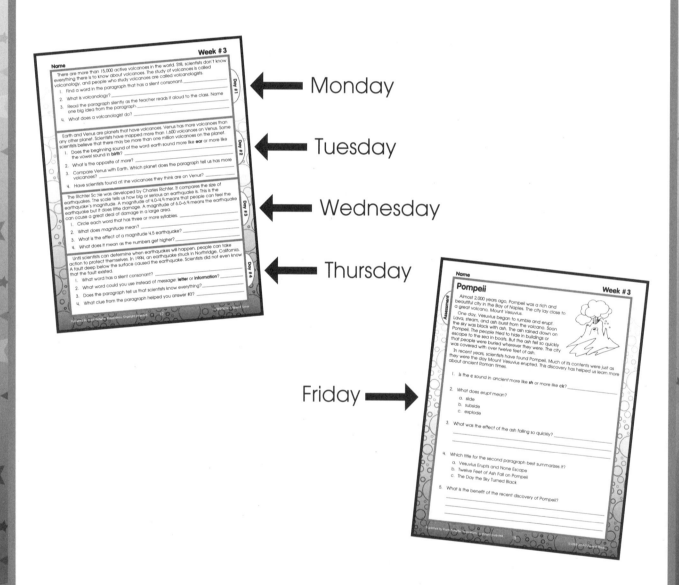

Monday

Tuesday

Wednesday

Thursday

Friday

Skills and concepts are reinforced throughout the book, and the book incorporates the style and syntax of standardized tests. The answer key reproduces each page, both daily practices and assessments, for ease in grading.

Reading Skills and Standards for Fourth Grade

Fluency

- ⊃ read text aloud with appropriate pacing, intonation, and expression
- ⊃ comprehend what is read as it is read (short time from reading to comprehension)
- ⊃ repeated practice in reading text aloud from student's "independent" level (approximately 1 in 20 words difficult for the reader)

Vocabulary

- ⊃ use word origins to find meaning of unknown words
- ⊃ use context to find meaning of unknown words
- ⊃ identify suffixes and prefixes to analyze the meaning of complex words
- ⊃ distinguish words with multiple meanings
- ⊃ effectively use reference tools such as a dictionary and thesaurus

Comprehension

- ⊃ identify main idea and supporting details
- ⊃ make predictions based on evidence in text (inferencing)
- ⊃ distinguish between fact and opinion
- ⊃ identify and analyze organizational structures in text (cause and effect, compare and contrast, chronological order)
- ⊃ identify the genre of a literary text
- ⊃ identify story elements (characters, setting, plot, problem, solution)
- ⊃ understand figurative language and its function in text (simile, metaphor, hyperbole, personification)

Published by Frank Schaffer Publications. Copyright protected.   0-7682-3214-7 *Read 4 Today*

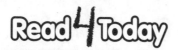

Building a Reading Environment

The reading environment is essential in fostering successful readers. When building a positive reading environment, think of students' physical, emotional, and cognitive needs.

Physical Environment

- Make the physical reading environment inviting and comfortable. Create a reading corner with comfortable chairs, floor pillows, a rug, enticing lighting, and so on.
- Give students access to a variety of texts by providing books, magazines, newspapers, and Internet access. Read signs, ads, posters, menus, pamphlets, labels, boxes, and more!
- Provide regularly scheduled independent reading time in class. Encourage students to read at home. They can read to a younger sibling, or read anything of interest, such as comic books, children's and sports magazines, chapter books, and so on.
- Set a positive example. Make sure students see you reading along with them!

Emotional Environment

- Learn about students' reading habits, preferences, strengths, and weaknesses, and then provide books that address these issues.
- Help students create connections with text. Facilitate connections by activating prior knowledge, examining personal meaning, and respecting personal reflections.
- Give students the opportunity to choose books to read. This gives them a sense of ownership, helping to engage them in the text and sustain interest.
- Create a safe environment for exploring and trying new things. Foster a feeling of mutual respect for reading abilities and preferences.
- Require that students read at an appropriate reading level. Text in any content area, including leisure reading, should not be too easy or too difficult.
- Get all students to participate in reading, no matter what their reading level. Try not to alienate slower readers. Give them time to finish before moving on or asking questions.
- Be enthusiastic about reading! Talk about books you love, and share your reading experiences and habits. Your attitudes about reading are contagious!

Cognitive Environment

- No matter the grade level, read aloud to students every day. Reading aloud not only provides a good example, it also lets students practice their listening skills.
- Help students build their vocabularies to make reading more successful. Create word walls, personal word lists, mini-dictionaries, and graphic organizers.
- Read for different purposes. Reading a novel requires different skills than reading an instructions manual. Teach students the strategies needed to comprehend these texts.
- Encourage students to talk about what and how they read. Use journal writing, literature circles, class discussions, conferences, conversations, workshops, seminars, and more.
- Writing and reading are inherently linked. Students can examine their own writing through reading and examine their reading skills by writing. Whenever possible, facilitate the link between reading and writing.

Skills and Concepts   Odd-numbered weeks

week 1—page 13
beginning sounds
compound words
consonant blends
rhyming
synonyms
homographs
onomatopoeia
cause and effect
context clues

week 3—page 17
silent consonants
beginning sounds
syllables
antonyms
synonyms
big idea
compare and contrast
cause and effect
details
summarizing with title

week 5—page 21
vowel sounds
contractions
beginning and ending sounds
synonyms
predicting outcomes
supporting details
cause and effect

week 7—page 25
contractions
ending sounds
middle sounds
compound words
author's intention/purpose
author's feelings
supporting details

week 9—page 29
prefixes
syllables
compound words
beginning sounds
synonyms
antonyms
details
idioms

week 11—page 33
consonant sounds
ending sounds
vowel sounds
antonyms
synonyms
details
making predictions
context clues

week 13—page 37
vowel sounds (silent)
consonant blends
ending sounds
synonyms
details
author's purpose

week 15—page 41
beginning sounds
syllables
vowel sounds
middle sounds
prefixes
synonyms
main idea
math figuring

week 17—page 45
middle sound/vowel sounds
beginning/ending sounds
contractions
synonyms
context clues
making predictions
cause and effect

week 19—page 49
consonant digraphs
contractions
consonant sounds
beginning/ending sounds
middle sounds
alliteration
synonyms
sequence
author's intention
compare and contrast
details

week 21—page 53
beginning sounds
vowel sounds
compound words
prefixes
synonyms
supporting details
author's intention/purpose
context clues

week 23—page 57
rhyme
syllables
digraph **gh**
homophones
main idea
synonyms

Published by Frank Schaffer Publications. Copyright protected.   0-7682-3214-7 *Read 4 Today*

Skills and Concepts   Odd-numbered weeks

week 25—page 61
vowel sounds
beginning sounds
context clues
homophones
homographs
compare and contrast
reading in content area: math

week 27—page 65
contractions
vowel blends
compound words
synonyms
compare and contrast
context clues
main subject
prefixes

week 29—page 69
syllables
compound words
silent consonants
homophones
synonyms
context clues
author's feelings
descriptive phrases
cause and effect

week 31—page 73
middle sounds
consonant blends
vowel blends
prefixes
homophones
antonyms
main idea
context clues

week 33—page 77
beginning sounds
ending sounds
context clues
main idea/subject
compare and contrast

week 35—page 81
consonant sounds
beginning sounds
middle sounds/vowel sounds
synonyms
compare and contrast
choosing a title
topic sentence
details chart

week 37—page 85
silent letters
ending sounds
vowel pairs
suffixes
synonyms
cause and effect
context clues
predicting outcomes

week 39—page 89
homophones
middle sounds
plurals
prefixes
synonyms
main subject
title for paragraph

Published by Frank Schaffer Publications. Copyright protected.   0-7682-3214-7 *Read 4 Today*

Skills and Concepts

Even-numbered weeks

Skills and Concepts   Even-numbered weeks

week 26—page 63

title clues
opening sentence
fact and opinion
details
reading in content area: science

week 28—page 67

title clues
opinion
cause and effect
context clues
details
conflict
character

week 30—page 71

title clues
context clues
setting
compare and contrast
cause and effect
author's feelings
character details

week 32—page 75

title clues
details
cause and effect
context clues
reading in content area: math
character's motivations

week 34—page 79

genre
character's motivations
details
setting
context clues
moral of the story
cause and effect

week 36—page 83

title clues
details
making connections
context clues
making comparisons

week 38—page 87

title clues
details
author's feelings
cause and effect
predicting outcomes
opinion

week 40—page 91

title clues
author's feelings
context clues
comparison chart
details
making comparisons
opinion

Published by Frank Schaffer Publications. Copyright protected.
0-7682-3214-7 *Read 4 Today*

Scope and Sequence

Skill / Concept	1	2	3	4	5	6	7	8	9	10	11	12	13	14	15	16	17	18	19	20
beginning sounds:	•		•		•				•						•		•		•	
middle sounds:			•		•		•				•		•						•	
ending sounds:			•		•		•				•		•				•		•	
consonant pairs/blends:	•		•										•						•	
vowel pairs:							•								•			•		
compound words:	•								•		•									
synonyms:	•		•		•				•		•		•		•		•		•	
antonyms:			•						•		•									
prefixes:									•											
syllables:			•												•					
silent letters:			•										•							
homographs:	•						•													
homophones:											•									
main idea:	•		•		•															
cause and effect:	•	•	•	•	•	•						•					•	•	•	•
compare and contrast:				•		•				•		•		•		•	•	•		
context clues:	•	•		•						•		•	•							
title clues:		•				•		•		•		•	•	•	•	•	•	•		•
character:		•		•				•		•		•		•				•		•
conflict and resolution:										•		•		•						
genre:						•				•			•							
details:	•		•		•			•	•		•		•		•	•			•	•
making predictions:					•						•									
contractions:					•		•			•							•		•	
author's feelings:				•		•	•	•												
author's intention/purpose:							•					•		•			•		•	
opinion:				•									•							
setting:									•	•		•		•						
rhyming:	•														•	•				
math:																•			•	
sequencing:													•						•	
other:	•	•	•	•	•	•	•	•	•	•	•	•	•	•	•	•	•	•	•	•

T = Weekly Test   • Indicates Skill or Concept Included and/or Tested

11

0-7682-3214-7 *Read 4 Today*

Scope and Sequence

Skill	21	22	23	24	25	26	27	28	29	30	31	32	33	34	35	36	37	38	39	40
beginning sounds	•				•	•							•		•	•				
middle sounds		•									•				•				•	
ending sounds													•				•			
consonant pairs/blends			•				•								•		•		•	
vowel pairs											•				•		•			
compound words	•						•		•		•						•		•	
synonyms	•		•				•		•						•				•	
antonyms									•								•			
prefixes	•								•		•						•			
syllables			•								•									
silent letters							•													
homographs			•		•						•								•	
homophones			•		•						•		•						•	
main idea							•		•											
cause and effect			•			•		•		•		•		•	•	•	•	•		•
compare and contrast		•			•		•			•					•	•	•	•		•
context clues		•			•		•			•		•	•	•		•	•			•
title clues				•				•		•		•	•	•				•		•
character								•		•						•	•	•		
conflict and resolution																				
genre				•										•						
details	•	•		•		•	•	•		•		•	•	•	•	•	•	•	•	•
making predictions																				•
contractions					•			•												
author's feelings				•		•	•		•	•		•								
author's intention/purpose	•	•																		
opinion		•							•											•
setting	•	•								•				•						
rhyming			•									•								
math		•			•							•								
sequencing			•				•													•
other	•	•	•	•	•	•	•	•	•	•	•	•	•	•	•	•	•	•	•	•

T = Weekly Test   • Indicates Skill or Concept Included and/or Tested

0-7682-3214-7 Read 4 Today

Tanner and Nick were roller-skating down the sidewalk. Nick hit a stone and fell. His knees and hands slammed into the ground. It was a good thing he was wearing kneepads. His hands were another story.

1. Find a word in the paragraph that starts with a silent consonant. _____

2. What is another word you could use instead of *slammed*? _____

3. What was the effect of Nick hitting a stone while roller-skating? _____
   _____

4. What happened to Nick's hands? _____

Only three problems out of his thirty-two were done. For the past half-hour Dan had been looking at the page and daydreaming. "Hey, pass your paper up," said Joe. "Mrs. Willis just asked for our work."

1. Find a word that is made up of two other words. _____

2. What is another way to say *half hour*? _____

3. *Pass* is a homograph, a word that can be used different ways. Circle the use here that is used the same way as in our paragraph: "I passed the test anyway!" or "Pass me the butter."

4. Who is Mrs. Willis? _____

Bonnie Butterfly flew through the air. She could see for miles. Bonnie was exhausted and hungry and she wanted to land. She felt very comfortable flying, but landing was still hard for her. She caught sight of a patch of delicious-looking flowers. "Oh dear," she thought. "Do I dare land there?"

1. Circle the word in the paragraph that has the same consonant blend as *angry*.
2. What does *exhausted* mean? _____
3. What does *dare* mean to Bonnie? Did another butterfly dare her to land there?
   _____

4. Bonnie Butterfly has only just learned how to fly. Circle the sentence that tells you that.

Have you ever listened to the sweet strings of symphony violins? Perhaps you have heard the light melody of the flutes. Or maybe you have heard the ping of harp strings. The musicians in the orchestra are seated in special places to make the music sound just right.

1. Circle the words that rhyme with *fight*.

2. What is a symphony? _____

3. Some words sound like what they mean. As your teacher reads the paragraph out loud, circle the word or words that sound like what they mean.

4. Is a symphony the same as an orchestra? _____

Salt and Pepper

Salt and Pepper were born in the same month and lived together at Peterson's Pet Shop. Salt was a white kitten whose cage sat in the front window beside a black puppy named Pepper. The two were best friends.

One day, Manuel and his father came into Peterson's Pet Shop to purchase a kitten. Manuel chose Salt because she was so playful.

Several weeks later, Lorinda and her mother stopped by the pet shop to look at the puppies. "Oh, Mama," said Lorinda. "This little black puppy has such beautiful eyes, and he likes me already."

"He seems great," said her mother. "I hope he gets along with our neighbor Manuel's new white kitten."

"Oh, I think they'll be best friends," Lorinda replied. "Won't they be cute together? Just like salt and pepper!"

1. Find a word with the suffix -ful. What does the suffix mean?

   _____

2. What word could you use instead of purchase?

   _____

3. What was the effect of Salt and Pepper living next to each other in the pet shop?

   _____

   _____

   _____

4. Is Lorinda right when she says, "Oh, I think they'll be best friends"? What clues from the story helped you answer that question?

   _____

   _____

   _____

5. Why did it make sense for the kitten to be named Salt and the puppy to be named Pepper?

   _____

   _____

   _____

Tree Needs

Dave was helping his dad plant some ash trees in the yard.

1. What does the title tell us about what the subject of the passage might be?
   _____

2. Does the title say anything specific about the subject?_____

3. What does the opening sentence tell us about who is in this passage?
   _____

4. What are they doing? _____

Day #1

Dave picked up the shovel and walked over to the place where they had laid out the last tree. He pushed the shovel into the ground. The point wouldn't go in, so Dave tried jumping on the shovel.

"Dad, the ground here is so hard I can't get the blade in the soil," said Dave.

1. Is there a problem in this passage? If so, what is it?_____
   _____

2. Does a character try to solve the problem?_____

3. If so, what does the character do? _____

4. Did you find out more about the subject we guessed from the title? _____

Day #2

Mr. Ruiz came and looked at the ground. "We may need to find another place to plant this tree," he said. "Like all plants, trees need four things—sunlight, air, water, and good soil. While there is plenty of sunlight, this place may lack the soil, water, and air that the tree needs."

1. Has a new character entered the story? If so, what is that character's name?
   _____

2. What is the effect of the problem? _____

3. Did you find out more about the subject we guessed from the title? _____

4. If so, what have you discovered? _____

Day #3

Mr. Ruiz slowly walked around the yard. Every once in a while, he poked the point of the shovel into the dirt to test the soil. Soon the shovel blade sliced easily into the dirt. "I think we just found a new home for this last tree," said Mr. Ruiz. "Do you see this soil? It's loose and black, which means there are lots of nutrients in it. And with the soil being loose, the water and air can easily drain down to the tree's roots."

1. Did the characters solve the problem? _____

2. If so, how did they solve it?_____

3. Were there any more details about the subject in the last paragraph? If so, what?_____

4. Was this a story or a science article? _____

Day #4

1. Do the title and opening paragraph remind you of a fairy tale you know? If so, which fairy tale?

_____

The Goldilocks Report

At 5:05 p.m., we were called to the home of a Mr. and Mrs. Bear.

2. Who is involved in this story?_____

_____

_____

They had been out for the day. Upon returning home, they found the lock on their door had been broken. Officer Paws and I went into the house. We found that food had been stolen and a chair had been broken.

3. What is the problem in the story? _____

_____

_____

_____

Paws searched the back yard while I went upstairs. I found a person asleep in a small bed. The subject was a female human with curly, blonde hair. She was unknown to the Bear family. The human claimed her name was Goldilocks. She could not prove that fact. She will be questioned at the police station.

4. How is the solution to the problem in this story different from the end of the story in the fairy tale?

_____

_____

_____

5. Who is in this story but is not in the fairy tale? _____

_____

_____

_____

There are more than 15,000 active volcanoes in the world. Still, scientists don't know everything there is to know about volcanoes. The study of volcanoes is called volcanology, and people who study volcanoes are called volcanologists.

1. Find a word in the paragraph that has a silent consonant._____

2. What is volcanology? _____

3. Read the paragraph silently as the teacher reads it aloud to the class. Name one big idea from the paragraph._____

_____

4. What does a volcanologist do? _____

Earth and Venus are planets that have volcanoes. Venus has more volcanoes than any other planet. Scientists have mapped more than 1,600 volcanoes on Venus. Some scientists believe that there may be more than one million volcanoes on the planet.

1. Does the beginning sound of the word *earth* sound more like **ear** or more like the vowel sound in **birth**? _____

2. What is the opposite of *more*? _____

3. Compare Venus with Earth. Which planet does the paragraph tell us has more volcanoes? _____

4. Have scientists found all the volcanoes they think are on Venus? _____

The Richter Scale was developed by Charles Richter. It compares the size of earthquakes. The scale tells us how big or serious an earthquake is. This is the earthquake's magnitude. A magnitude of 4.0–4.9 means that people can feel the earthquake but it does little damage. A magnitude of 6.0–6.9 means the earthquake can cause a great deal of damage in a large area.

1. Circle each word that has three or more syllables. _____

2. What does *magnitude* mean? _____

3. What is the effect of a magnitude 4.5 earthquake? _____

4. What does it mean as the numbers get higher?_____

Until scientists can determine when earthquakes will happen, people can take action to protect themselves. In 1994, an earthquake struck in Northridge, California. A fault deep below the surface caused the earthquake. Scientists did not even know that the fault existed.

1. What word has a silent consonant? _____

2. What word could you use instead of *message*: **letter** or **information**?_____

3. Does the paragraph tell us that scientists know everything?_____

4. What clue from the paragraph helped you answer #3? _____

Pompeii

Almost 2,000 years ago, Pompeii was a rich and beautiful city in the Bay of Naples. The city lay close to a great volcano, Mount Vesuvius.

One day, Vesuvius began to rumble and erupt. Lava, steam, and ash burst from the volcano. Soon the sky was black with ash. The ash rained down on Pompeii. The people tried to hide in buildings or escape to the sea in boats. But the ash fell so quickly that people were buried wherever they were. The city was covered with over twelve feet of ash.

In recent years, scientists have found Pompeii. Much of its contents were just as they were the day Mount Vesuvius erupted. This discovery has helped us learn more about ancient Roman times.

1. Is the **c** sound in *ancient* more like **sh** or more like **ck**? _____

2. What does *erupt* mean?

   a. slide

   b. subside

   c. explode

3. What was the effect of the ash falling so quickly? _____

   _____

   _____

4. Which title for the second paragraph best summarizes it?

   a. Vesuvius Erupts and None Escape

   b. Twelve Feet of Ash Fall on Pompeii

   c. The Day the Sky Turned Black

5. What is the benefit of the recent discovery of Pompeii?

   _____

   _____

   _____

The Underground Railroad

The Underground Railroad wasn't a railroad at all. It was a group of people who helped slaves escape to freedom. Those in charge of the escape effort were often called "conductors." The people escaping were known as "passengers." And the places where the escaping slaves stopped for help were often called "stations."

1. Cover the opening sentence with your hand. What do you think the title alone tells you about what the subject of the selection might be? _____
2. Does the opening sentence support or contradict your guess? _____
3. What is the subject of this selection? _____
4. What does the opening paragraph tell us about who is involved? _____

Day #1

Like a train ride, the Underground Railroad moved people along. Those who escaped often followed routes that had been laid out by others before them. However, unlike a train ride, some routes went underground through dirt tunnels without any sort of tracks.

1. Does this paragraph make a comparison? _____
2. How is the subject like the thing it's compared with? _____
3. How is the subject unlike the thing it's compared with? _____
4. How does this paragraph make you feel? _____

Day #2

Escaping slaves had to be certain that they could find their way. They needed food and water to make the journey. Conductors often helped with this. One of the most famous Underground Railroad conductors was Harriet Tubman. She had escaped slavery herself. Another famous conductor was Levi Coffin.

1. What part of the subject does this paragraph focus on? _____
2. What was their job? _____
3. Did you find out any names of conductors? _____
4. What details did you find out about any of the conductors? _____

Day #3

Experts disagree about how well the Underground Railroad was organized. Still, it is believed that the system helped thousands of slaves reach freedom between 1830 and 1865.

1. What was the problem the Underground Railroad was trying to solve?
   _____
2. What new details did you learn? _____
3. How many years did the Underground Railroad operate? _____
4. Imagine traveling the Underground Railroad. Did you imagine yourself as the slave or the conductor? _____

Day #4

Quilts Reflect a Culture

1. A quilt is like a sandwich: fabric as the "bread" and cotton filling as the "peanut butter." What practical reason would a person have to make a quilt?

   a. to stay warm

   b. to use as kindling

   c. to eat

Many African women knew how to sew when they came to America as slaves. They were skillful seamstresses. Sometimes they sold for as much as $1,000 on the slavery block.

2. Why do you think seamstresses had such high value? _____

   _____

Some slaves made quilts for their owners. They used the scraps from those quilts to make quilts for their own families. Those quilts often told the story of their families. They're called story quilts.

3. Did quilts have only practical purposes for the slaves who made them? What clues from the paragraph helped you answer that question?

   _____

   _____

A slave named Elizabeth Keckley supported 17 people by sewing. In 1855, she made enough money to buy freedom for herself and her son. That freedom cost her $1,200. She moved to Washington, D.C. There she sewed for President Lincoln's wife. She made a quilt that probably used scraps from Mrs. Lincoln's gowns.

4. Answer question 2 again using the information you just learned.

   _____

   _____

5. What do you think is the most surprising or interesting fact in the last paragraph?

   _____

One day Jimmy raced into the kitchen and announced, "I am no longer eating anything green! I just found out that all green food was developed to turn humans into aliens. So I won't be able to eat anything like peas or broccoli!"

"I'm so sorry to hear that, Jimmy," replied his mom. "I guess you won't be having any key lime pie or mint chocolate chip ice cream for dessert tonight."

1. Circle all words that have the same vowel sound as *meat/meet*.
2. What word could you use instead of *announced*? _____
3. Try to predict Jimmy's reaction to what his mom says. What do you think it is?
   _____
4. Why did Jimmy say that all green food was developed to turn humans into aliens? _____

Tara was hungry. She'd been playing basketball for two hours. She ran inside and saw some cookies her grandmother had just baked sitting on the counter.

1. There is one contraction in the paragraph. If you undo it, what does it say?
   _____
2. How many minutes long is one hour? _____
3. As your teacher reads the paragraph, try to predict what Tara will do at the end. Will she
   a. grab two cookies?   b. grab an apple?   c. put the cookies away?
4. What detail from the story gave you the answer for #3? _____

Ashanti passed a pet store on the way home from school. In the window, she saw a cute puppy. Ashanti put her hand on the window near the puppy. It jumped at her hand and licked the window, wagging its tail.

1. Circle all the words that begin and end with the same sound.
2. What does wagging look like? Does it mean that the puppy is **happy** or **angry**?
   _____
3. As the teacher reads the story, try to predict what happens at the end.
   Did Ashanti
      a. go in to see the puppy?   b. run away in fright?   c. drive a car?
4. What detail from the story helped you answer #3? _____

"Let's clean up," said Mrs. Perez. "It's nearly time to go home." Andre hurried to the pet corner to take care of the hamster. Just as he was fastening the door to the hamster cage, the fire alarm rang. The teacher and children quickly left the building. The hamster looked at the half-closed door.

1. What does each contraction say when you undo it? _____
2. Give two words other than *hurried* that describe moving quickly. _____
3. Try to predict what happens. Does the hamster...
   a. close the door?   b. escape?   c. go to sleep?
4. What clues helped you answer #3? Was it something you know outside the paragraph? _____

Assessment

The Storm

Willie sat in front of the TV while a storm raged outside his house. The wind howled, the rain came down in buckets, and thunder boomed loudly. The high winds knocked down a huge oak tree down the street. The tree fell on top of the street's power line, cutting the electricity to Willie's house. Willie found a flashlight and turned it on.

Willie shone the flashlight ahead of him as he walked down the hallway. As he entered the kitchen, the flashlight batteries died. The room became inky black. Willie ran into the wall and stubbed his toe. He hollered and jumped on one foot. He bumped into the table, which knocked over his marble jar. Marbles scattered all over the table and floor.

Muttsie, Willie's dog, jumped up at the noise and ran toward Willie's voice. The dog skidded on the marbles. She flew across the floor into her dog dishes, spilling water and food everywhere.

Willie's cat, Kitty, was showered with water from the spilled dog dish. She jumped to the safety of the counter. She landed on the edge of a cookie sheet sticking out of the dish rack. The cookie sheet flipped over, taking the contents of the dish rack with it.

1. Find the word that sounds like *tow*. _____

2. What does *scattered* mean?

    a. stayed in a clump

    b. spread out quickly

    c. moved in an orderly line

3. List one cause and its effect for each paragraph.

_____

_____

_____

_____

4. Predict what happens to the pots, plates, and silverware in the dish rack.

_____

_____

5. What lesson could Willie learn from this experience?

_____

_____

_____

Name

A Night in Texas

Dear Hailey,

We are in Austin, Texas. You would never believe what I saw tonight.

1. What does the title tell us about where and when this selection takes place?
    _____
2. What kind of writing is this? _____
3. Does the opening give us any more hints about what the selection will be about? If so, what? _____
4. Does it sound like the author is excited or bored by what he or she has to say?
    _____

Day #1

   We were in a restaurant by the Congress Avenue Bridge. As the sun was going down, I saw a cloud moving around by the bridge. The cloud was bats! The bats live under the bridge where it is dark. The sun does not shine under the bridge, but when the sun started to go down, all of those bats woke up.

1. What new details did you learn about where the author is? _____
2. What is the thing the author is reporting? _____
3. Does the author sound amazed or humdrum? _____
4. Did you learn any more details about what time of night it is? If so, what?
    _____

Day #2

   They were hungry. The waitress said over a million Mexican free-tailed bats live under the Congress Avenue Bridge. Another waitress said the bats were really good because they eat over 10,000 pounds of insects EVERY NIGHT! I weigh about 60 pounds, so that's like eating enough insects to make about 170 of me.

1. What new details did you learn about the bats? _____
2. What new details did you learn about the author? _____
3. Does the author make a comparison in this paragraph? _____
4. If so, what is the comparison? _____

Day #3

   Boy, maybe we need some of those bats by our house. I sure hated all of those mosquitoes that were trying to eat us last week. Well, I've got to go. Don't get too "batty" without me!

                                            Sincerely,
                                            Mikaela

1. Is the author a boy or a girl? _____
2. What connection does the author make between her night in Texas and her life at home? _____
3. Are mosquitoes a problem in warm weather where you live? If so, would you like a cloud of bats living near you? _____
4. Why does the author include the last sentence? _____

Day #4

Assessment

1. Glance down at the reading. What kind of writing is this?

_____

Hopi Prayer
Anonymous

Come here, Thunder, and look!
Come here, Cold, and see it rain!

2. Does the title tell you the name of the person who wrote the Hopi prayer?

_____

_____

Thunder strikes and makes it hot.
All seeds grow when it is hot.

3. What kind of weather does the prayer describe?

_____

_____

Corn in blossom,
Beans in blossom,
Your face on garden looks,
Watermelon plant, muskmelon plant.
Your face on garden looks.
Aha-aha-ehe-ihe.

4. What season does this poem talk about?

    a. winter
    b. spring
    c. summer

5. What is another good title for this poem?

    a. Summer Harvest
    b. Thunderstorms
    c. Growing Fruits

A fierce warrior, Crazy Horse was known as a Lakota tribe member who would not give up. Born in 1849, Crazy Horse worked hard to keep the Native American way of life from disappearing. He did not want to lose the customs of his tribe.

1. Turn *would not* into a contraction. _____

2. What does *fierce* mean? _____

3. Why did the author write this paragraph: to tell us about Crazy Horse or to tell us that the Lakota were in danger of losing their customs? _____

4. What did Crazy Horse work hard to do? _____

Native Americans respect the earth. They try to live in harmony with nature. Native Americans use the earth's gifts wisely. These gifts are called natural resources. Natural resources include the land, plants, animals, water, and minerals.

1. Circle the words that end with a *y* that have an **i** sound. Put a line through words that end with a *y* that have an **ee** sound.

2. What does *live in harmony with nature* mean?_____

3. What does the author of the paragraph appreciate about Native Americans?

_____

4. What are natural resources? _____

At one time, huge herds of buffalo lived on the plains. The Native Americans followed the buffalo. These people needed the animals for their survival. The animals were used for meat. The hides were used for clothing. The bones were used for tools and jewelry. The tendons were used to string bows.

1. When the author uses the word *live,* is the *i* pronounced like the *i* in the word **hive** or the word **river**?_____

2. *Hide* is a word that can be used to talk about the skin of an animal. Use *hide* a different way in a sentence. _____

3. Did Native Americans hunt the buffalo just for fun?_____

4. What details from the story gave you the answer to #3? _____

Wilma Mankiller was born in 1945. She is a Cherokee from Oklahoma. She became principal chief of the Cherokee Nation in 1985. She has worked hard for improved health care and civil rights. Mankiller believes in an old Cherokee saying about being of good mind. She says today this is called "positive thinking."

1. Find a word that is a compound—two words put together to make a new word. _____

2. What does *improved* mean?_____

3. What is another way of saying *positive thinking*? _____

4. What is the author trying to do in this paragraph: **give us information** or **make us laugh**? _____

Assessment

Medicine Men and Their Herbs

Did you know Native Americans use plants as medicine? Medicine men use herbs and other plants to help cure illnesses. They gather the plants and dry them to make teas or grind dried herbs into a paste by mixing them with water. They use all parts of the plants in their herbal remedies: the stems, the leaves, the flowers, the bark, and the roots.

If you looked in a medicine man's medicine cabinet you might find garlic cloves for insect stings. Or you might find sunflower seeds and roots to soothe a blister. Slippery elm tea was used for curing sore throats. Dandelion tea was good for heartburn. If you had a problem with dandruff, the medicine man might give you a dose of sword fern tea. He would use pinesap to heal cuts. Witch hazel works on sprains and bruises. He might suggest you chew spruce pine cones for your sore throat. If you couldn't get rid of a headache, he'd probably give you willow bark. Willow bark contains salicyclic acid. That's the main ingredient in aspirin. Many of these herbs are available today in drugstores. You might want to keep some willow bark on hand.

1. What do these words have in common?

   sunflower, heartburn, headache, drugstores

   _____

   _____

2. What is a paste?_____

   _____

3. What part of a sunflower plant can be used to soothe a blister?

   _____

   _____

4. What do you think the author was trying to do in this article?

   a. tell how medicine men make tea

   b. tell how medicine men use plants

   c. tell you how to become a medicine man

5. How is willow bark like aspirin?

   _____

   _____

   _____

The Story of the Cherokee Rose

In 1838, the government of the United States made the Cherokees move from their homes in Georgia and other states to what was then called the Indian Territory. That land is now the state of Oklahoma.

1. What clues does the title give us about the subject of this article? _____
   _____
2. Does this paragraph tell us anything about who the Cherokees were? _____
3. Does this paragraph tell us anything about the rose in the title?_____
4. How long ago did this story take place? _____

Day #1

The Cherokees had to walk about a thousand miles, and they often did not have enough food or water. Many hundreds of them died. The mothers felt so sad that some of them could not take care of their children.

1. How did the Cherokees get to Indian Territory? _____
2. Does the author include any opinions in this paragraph? _____
3. Who is feeling sad in this paragraph? _____
4. This trip is called the Trail of Tears. What clues tell you why? _____
   _____

Day #2

The old men of the tribe asked the Great One for a sign that would make the mothers feel better and make them strong enough to take care of their children.

1. Who in the tribe came up with a solution to the problem?_____
2. What solution did the tribe come up with for the mothers? _____
   _____
3. Is the Great One **a religious figure** or **the tallest Cherokee**? _____
4. If you were the Great One, what kind of sign would you send to make the mothers feel better and be stronger?_____
   _____

Day #3

The Great One promised that where a mother's tear fell, a flower would grow. That flower is called the Cherokee rose. It is white, and that color stands for the mothers' tears. The center of the flower is gold. That is a symbol of the gold that was taken from the tribes' land. The seven leaves on the rose's stem stand for the seven groups of people that walked along the Trail of Tears.

1. Which paragraph told you what the Cherokee rose is?_____
2. How does the story say the Cherokee rose comes about?_____
3. What are the different parts of the rose and what are they symbols of? You may want to make a chart. _____
4. How does this story make you feel?_____

Day #4

1. Without looking back on your earlier work, what do you remember about the Trail of Tears?

_____

_____

The Trail of Tears

The ancient Cherokee were hunters and farmers. They lived in the area that we know as the Appalachian Mountains of Georgia. But in 1829, white settlers found gold on this land. They went to the United States government and asked that the Cherokee be forced to leave the land, hoping they would then get the rights to it.

2. Why did the settlers want the Cherokee gone? _____

_____

_____

_____

A new law called the Indian Removal Act of 1830 was passed. The law stated that all Native Americans east of the Mississippi would be moved. They would have to go live on an Indian territory in the west, an area in what is now Oklahoma.

3. Were the settlers successful? _____

Some agreed to go, but most would not leave their land. Starting in the spring of 1838, the army gathered the Cherokee together. The people were held in forts like prisoners. Within one month, the first group of Cherokee was forced to leave Georgia. They marched over 1,000 miles to the new land. Some people had horses and wagons. Most people walked. The trip lasted many months. Hundreds died, either during the march or once they got to the land. There was no shelter or food at the territory. The last group of Cherokee arrived on the Indian Territory in March of 1839. In all, almost 17,000 Cherokee were forced to move to the new land.

4. Did the Cherokee go willingly? _____

5. Which point of view do you agree with: that of the settlers or the Cherokee? Explain your answer.

_____

_____

_____

_____

_____

_____

Diego came down with the flu on Monday night, and his doctor told him to stay home from school for the rest of the week. She told him that he could do schoolwork on Thursday, but not to overdo it.

1. *Over* is a prefix that means "too much" or "more than usual." So what does *over + do* mean? _____

2. Which of the following phrases matches the doctor's advice to Diego: "Do schoolwork but take it easy" or "Be sure to do all your schoolwork"?

3. How many days was Diego home not doing schoolwork? _____

4. Is having the flu an excuse to ignore your schoolwork? _____

Day #1

Joe and Gabby needed information for their report on theropods. It was hard to find resources on this dinosaur. They decided not to get another topic. They would leave no stone unturned while looking for information.

1. Circle all the words with three syllables.

2. What are resources?_____

3. Are theropods common dinosaurs to study? What detail helps you answer that question? _____

4. What does "leave no stone unturned" mean? Will they turn over every stone they see to look for theropod fossils, or will they look for information everywhere?

_____

Day #2

Rebecca didn't finish her math homework last night. She played on the computer instead. She asked her mother to tell her teacher that she had been sick. Her mother told her that she would have to face the music herself.

1. Circle the word that is made up of two words put together.

2. What is one word that says what Rebecca asked her mother to do?_____

3. Did Rebecca make a good choice? Why or why not? _____

4. What does "face the music herself" mean? Will Rebecca's teacher play music in class, or must Rebecca accept the consequences of her actions?

_____

Day #3

One morning at school you see your friend looking dreamy-eyed. On her paper she has drawn hearts and flowers.

1. Does the beginning sound of *school* sound like the beginning sound of **skate** or **shoot**? _____

2. What is the opposite of *dreamy-eyed*? _____

3. Do you want to ask your friend about the reason for her behavior? Why or why not? _____

4. What do you think is going on with your friend? _____

Day #4

The Test

Assessment

Billy knew that he was in trouble...big trouble. Ms. Keaton, his teacher, had seen him cheating on his test. She hadn't said anything yet, but Billy knew that she'd seen him peek at the little piece of paper hidden in his hand. He chewed on his pencil for a minute and thought. He had to get rid of that paper. But how?

"Billy, if you are finished with your test, would you please come up here?" Billy nodded. His heart was pounding so hard that he couldn't speak. He bent down to tie one of his shoes. Could he stuff the paper in his shoe? No, Ms. Keaton was watching him...waiting for him.

Billy swallowed hard. If only he had studied last night, instead of watching that TV show! Then, on the bus this morning, he decided to write down a few science facts on a piece of paper and hide it in the palm of his hand. It had been a crazy idea, and now he was going to pay for it.

Billy walked up slowly to Ms. Keaton's desk. In a flash, he had an idea! As he stood by her desk, he could let the paper fall into her wastebasket. Later, he could try to get it back again. It was a great idea!

Ms. Keaton smiled at Billy. "Since you finished first," she said, "I thought you might like to help me set up our science experiment." Billy was stunned. What luck! Ms. Keaton hadn't seen his little piece of paper. Now all he had to do was get it into the wastebasket. As he nodded, he opened his hand. The paper fluttered down. A sudden breeze from an open window made it float down to Ms. Keaton's feet.

"Billy, you dropped this," said Ms. Keaton. She picked it up. Then she looked at it more closely. "What exactly is this?" she asked, looking worried.

1. List two words that rhyme with *loose*. _____

2. Find two words in paragraph 5 that could be synonyms.

    _____

3. Mark each of these parts of the story with an **E** for an important event or **D** for a story detail.

    _____ a. Billy watches television instead of studying.

    _____ b. Ms. Keaton calls Billy up to her desk.

    _____ c. Billy ties one of his shoes.

    _____ d. Billy's heart pounds.

    _____ e. Ms. Keaton picks up the paper.

4. Did Billy think it was a good idea to cheat on his test at the beginning of the story? Did he change his mind by the end?_____

5. What does "pay for it" mean?

    _____

Samantha's Birthday

Let's see how the different members of Samantha's family celebrated her birthday.

1. What does the title tell us about the subject of this selection?_____
2. Does the first sentence support your guess?_____
3. Who else will be in this story? _____
4. Does it tell us which birthday this is? _____

I knew it would be a great day from the minute I woke up. Piled beside my bed was a stack of presents. I jumped out of bed. I was so excited. When I came downstairs carrying the presents, everyone shouted, "Happy birthday!"

1. Who is the writer of this paragraph? _____
2. What is the first thing that happened after Samantha woke up?

   _____
3. How does the writer feel? _____
4. Where does this paragraph take place?_____

Before Samantha woke up, I left her presents beside her bed. I knew she would like the surprise from her father and me. When we saw Samantha on the stairs, we surprised her by saying, "Happy birthday!"

1. Who is the writer of this paragraph? _____
2. What clues helped you answer #1?_____
3. What two things did the writer do to surprise Samantha?

   _____
4. Does this paragraph tell us what kind of presents Samantha gets? _____

I bought Samantha a book about dinosaurs for her birthday. Mom and Dad let me do extra chores to earn the money. I had to wake up early to surprise her but it was worth it to see her face when we all said, "Happy birthday!"

1. Who is the writer of this paragraph? _____
2. What clues helped you answer #1?_____
3. Does this paragraph tell us what kind of presents Samantha gets? _____
4. What was difficult for the writer of this passage to do? _____

   _____

1. Glance down at the reading. What type of writing is it?

   a. a poem

   b. religious writings

   c. directions

Putting It All Together

Juanita bought a dinosaur-shaped table as a birthday present for her little brother.

2. What does the first sentence tell us about the main character?

   _____

   _____

The entire table came in a box that was almost flat. Before she started putting the table together, Juanita took out the pieces and read the directions.

3. Have you learned what the title is about? If so, what?

   _____

   _____

Directions:

   1. Check to be sure you have all the pieces:
      one tabletop, four table legs, eight small screws,
      and four large screws.

   2. Snap the table legs into the tabletop holes.

   3. Screw in the large screws under the tabletop to hold
      the legs tight.

   4. Screw the small screws into the tabletop where marked.

4. Why is it important for Juanita to be certain that she has all the pieces before she begins to put the table together?

   _____

   _____

5. Why is it important for directions to list instructions in the correct order?

   _____

   _____

   _____

Name _____

A tarantula is a big, hairy spider. You might have seen one in a pet shop that carries spiders and other unusual pets. In the United States, tarantulas live in the west, where it is hot and dry. During the day, tarantulas sleep in holes and other dark places. They come out at night to hunt for food.

1. What word has a *t* that is pronounced like **ch**? _____
2. Give antonyms for *big, hairy*. _____
3. If you visit a pet shop that carries unusual pets, what pet might you see?
   a. cat   b. canary   c. tarantula
4. What might happen if you stuck your hand in a dark hole in Arizona? _____
_____

Day #1

Tarantulas catch their food mostly by jumping on it and biting it. Smaller tarantulas eat insects. Larger ones eat mice and lizards. A tarantula's poison can kill the animals it hunts, but its poison cannot kill a human.

1. Circle the word that has an ending sound like the middle *t* in *tarantula*.
2. What is another word for "the animals it hunts"?
   a. prey   b. toast   c. pray
3. What information in this paragraph might make you feel better about meeting up with a tarantula? _____
4. What kills the animals a tarantula hunts? _____

Day #2

If you are bitten, you will soon know that a tarantula bite hurts only about as much as a bee sting. Its bite helps this spider protect itself. Tarantulas are shy spiders. They bite humans only if they feel threatened and cannot get away.

1. The *i* in *bite* is pronounced a hard **i**. How is the *i* in *bitten* pronounced? _____
2. What is another word the author could have used instead of *shy*? _____
3. Someone who has been bitten by a tarantula will
   a. jump in the air, dance, and scream.   b. feel a bite like a bee sting.
4. Poking or touching a tarantula might make it
   a. run away.   b. bite you.   c. run after you until it catches you.

Day #3

A tarantula has another way to protect itself. It can rub its hind legs together, which causes its stiff leg hairs to fly up in the air. Each tiny hair can make a hurtful skin or eye wound.

1. Circle all the words that have a long **i**.
2. Which meaning of *wound* is correct here: **wrapped around** or **injury**?
3. What details does the writer use to describe tarantula hairs? _____
4. If you got down on your knees to look closely at a tarantula that was rubbing its hind legs together, what might happen? _____

Day #4

Venus Flytrap

Kayla got a Venus flytrap for her birthday. She put it with her other plants on her windowsill. She watered all of her plants each day.

After a week, all of her plants looked fine except her gift. She decided that she needed more information on this plant, so she went to the library and found a book about the Venus flytrap.

She was surprised to find out that this plant was carnivorous, or meat-eating. No wonder it was not doing well! The book said that the Venus flytrap is a popular house plant. Each set of leaves stays open until an insect or piece of meat lands on the inside of the leaf. The two leaves close quickly, trapping the bait inside. After a leaf digests the meat, it dies. A new leaf grows to take the place of the dead leaf.

Now Kayla knows how to take care of her Venus flytrap.

1. Complete this sentence with a homophone of *week*: After a week the Venus flytrap was _____.

2. What does the word *carnivorous* mean?

   _____

   _____

   _____

3. What clues from the compound word in the name *Venus flytrap* tell you what it might eat?

   _____

4. Why did Kayla need to go to the library?

   _____

   _____

   _____

5. What do you think Kayla will do next?

   _____

   _____

   _____

   _____

Name

Week #12

Special Spiders

Myra watched a bug scamper across the sidewalk. Its little legs moved so quickly. "That's a cool spider!" said a voice.

Day #1

1. What does the title tell us about the topic of this selection?_____
2. What is the setting of the story? _____
3. How does Myra feel about the bug in the sidewalk? _____
4. Whose voice do you guess Myra hears: **the spider's** or a **friend's**? _____

Myra turned around and saw her friend Dave. "How do you know it is a spider?" Myra asked.
"It has eight legs," said Dave. "If you look really closely, you will see that it does not have antennae either."
"When did you get to know so much about spiders?" asked Myra.

Day #2

1. Whose voice did Myra hear?_____
2. List two characteristics of spiders._____
3. Is it easy to determine whether there are or are not antennae on a bug? Why or why not? _____
4. Would you like to look that closely at a bug? Why or why not? _____

"I just read a book about them," Dave answered. "Like insects, spiders are invertebrates. They have a hard outer shell called an exoskeleton. The exoskeleton protects the soft inside parts of their bodies. They also have special eyes that help them hunt. The part I found the most interesting is that the spider, horseshoe crab, and the scorpion all belong to the same group."

Day #3

1. How are insects and spiders similar? _____
2. What did Dave say was the most interesting thing about spiders?_____
   _____
3. How does Dave feel about spiders? _____
4. Do you feel the same way? Why or why not? _____

"You have learned so much that I'm surprised you didn't know the name of that spider," said Myra.
"Give me some time," smiled Dave. "I'm reading a book about identifying spiders right now."

Day #4

1. Does Dave know everything there is to know about spiders?_____
2. What clue helped you answer #1? _____
3. How did Dave get his information on spiders?_____
4. What are some other sources he could go to?_____

Assessment

1. What does the title tell you about the subject of this article?

    _____

Impressive Insects

Periodical cicadas take from 13 to 17 years to change from an egg to a nymph to an adult, and then they live only four to six weeks as an adult. All that work for so little time seems like such a shame.

2. Which sentence in the first paragraph is the author's opinion?

    _____

    _____

Green grapplers eat only live insects. They grab an insect with the claws on their six front legs and then eat it. Often their prey is heavier than they are. Could you eat a hamburger that's heavier than you are?

3. If you ate a hamburger that weighed ½ of a pound, how many burgers would you have to eat to eat more than you weigh?

    _____

You can't tell if a saddleback caterpillar is coming or going. One end is like the other end. It's symmetrical. It has matched pairs of poisonous horns. One pair is on one end; another pair is on the other end. If you see one coming, or going, don't touch it. It can sting.

4. What is unique about the saddleback caterpillar?

    _____

    _____

5. Did the article live up to the title? Which insect do you think is the most impressive?

    _____

    _____

    _____

    _____

April took her dog Tasha for a walk on the beach. What a beautiful day! Many people were out walking their dogs. Suddenly, a black cat stepped out from behind a rock. Tasha chased the cat.

1. Find a word with a silent **o**. _____
2. Give two other words you could use instead of *beautiful*._____
3. What detail tells us that the cat surprised Tasha? _____
   _____
4. In this paragraph, is the author trying to give us information or tell an entertaining story? _____

Day #1

Everyone seems to like Dan because he is always amiable.

1. Circle the word that has its final *e* pronounced.
2. What does *amiable* mean? _____
3. What clues in the sentence gave you the answer to #2? _____
   _____
4. Does the sentence tell us that everyone likes Dan?_____
   _____

Day #2

Each spring we plant seeds and wait eagerly for them to sprout. This year Mom planted bulbs. We made sure the soil was warm and there was no chance of frost. We visited the nursery where they raise and sell plants and bought some fertilizer to improve the soil. Now we're sure the plants will bloom into beautiful flowers.

1. Circle all the words that start with the consonant blend **spr**.
2. What is another word you could use instead of *sprout*?_____
3. Do they plant seeds and bulbs right away in the spring? Circle the detail that gives you the answer._____
4. List the three steps the author took to make sure the bulbs bloom. _____
   _____

Day #3

In the spring, a horse or donkey may have a foal. It may be a male, a colt, or a female, a filly. The ewes may give birth to lambs at this time too. It's fun to watch the baby animals try to stand while their new legs are still shaky, or wobbly. Near the barn, the goose is careful when tending her goslings, while the family's dog feeds her whelps.

1. Circle the word that starts with the same ending sound in *threw*.
2. What is another word for *whelps*? _____
3. As your teacher reads this selection out loud, imagine where it takes place. Tell us where. _____
4. What time of year do these animals have their babies? _____

Day #4

Strawberries Save the Day

Some Native American legends explain the creation of the world or how things came to be. There is a Cherokee legend about the creation of strawberries. Here is a version of the story.

The first man and woman on the earth quarreled. The woman was so angry afterward that she left her husband. He missed her terribly. He decided to go to look for her. No matter how fast he traveled, he couldn't catch her. The sun watched from above. He felt sorry for the man and decided to help him. The sun created raspberries and caused them to grow in the woman's path. The berries didn't tempt the woman. She continued on her journey. Then the sun created blueberries to grow in her path. Again the woman wasn't tempted. Next the sun created blackberries. That didn't work either. Finally the sun created strawberries. The woman stopped right away. She bent down to pick a berry. When she tasted it, she smiled. She liked them so much she was still eating when her husband caught up to her. He apologized, and she forgave him. The moral of this story: Always be kind to one another.

1. Find a word with a silent **p**. _____

2. What other word could you use instead of *quarreled*?

   _____

3. Put the events of the story in the correct sequence using the numbers 1, 2, and 3.

   a. _____ The woman liked the strawberries so much that she stopped to eat them, and the man caught up to her.

   b. _____ After a couple quarreled, the woman ran away and her husband followed her.

   c. _____ No matter how fast he traveled, the man couldn't catch up with the woman.

4. What is a legend? _____

   _____

5. Make up an alternative moral for this story. _____

   _____

Lazy Time

Sally and Ned are swaying slowly in the family swing.

1. What does the title tell us about the story?_____
2. What information does the opening sentence add? _____
3. Is there an image in the first sentence that supports or illustrates the title? _____
4. If so, what is it and how does it illustrate the title? _____
_____

The air is crisp. Sally puts her arm around Ned and snuggles into his shaggy body. Ned's tongue licks Sally's hand that lies on her blue-jeaned leg. They watch a sluggish ladybug crawl underneath a pile of old, brown leaves. One red leaf drifts to the top of the ladybug's leaf pile.

1. What time of year is it?_____
2. What clues helped you answer #1?_____
3. What or who do you think Ned is? _____
4. What clues helped you answer #3?_____

Ned's graying ears prick up as a southbound V of geese honks goodbye. The sky slowly turns from blue, to pink, to purple, to black.

The first star shines as Sally's mom calls her in to eat. Sally gives a last push as she slides out of the swing. She walks to the back door of the house. Ned leaps down.

1. What sounds can you hear in this selection? _____
2. Is Ned a puppy or an older dog?_____
3. What clues helped you answer #2?_____
4. How does Sally feel?_____

Ned barks once at a rabbit, and then chases after Sally. She smiles and rubs Ned's head as they walk into the warm house together.

1. What meal is Sally about to eat? _____
2. Did the title set up the story well?_____
3. List the words in all the selections that give a picture of laziness. _____
_____
4. What other title would work? _____

Assessment

1. This is a table of contents for a book. What does a table of contents tell you?

_____

A Year in My Life

CONTENTS

2. What time of year is it in the first three chapters? _____

3. What season is it in chapters 7–9? _____

4. Do you think chapter 13 is about the harvest festival of Thanksgiving or about the author harvesting food from a garden? What clues helped you answer that question?

_____

_____

_____

5. Is the book arranged thematically (by theme) or chronologically (by time)?

_____

_____

Numismatics, or coin collecting, is a very old hobby. It began long ago in other countries. It was not popular right away in America. Most Americans were too busy building a country out of a wilderness to think about collecting coins. It was not until about 1840 that Americans began to become serious coin collectors.

1. Circle all the words that start with a hard **c**.

2. What is numismatics? _____

3. What is the main idea of this paragraph? _____

4. Why did this hobby start so late in America? _____

In the United States, paper money was first issued in 1775. That year, the Continental Congress authorized the issue, or giving out, of paper money to finance the Revolutionary War. This "continental currency" soon came to be worth very little and fell out of use.

1. Circle the word with most syllables. How many syllables does it have?_____

2. In this paragraph, does *issue* mean **to give out** or **offspring**? _____

3. Why was the money called "continental currency"? _____

4. Has the United States always used paper money? _____

In 1865, the Secret Service was established to control counterfeit, or fake, money. At that time, about one-third of the money in circulation was counterfeit.

1. What sound does the *ei* in *counterfeit* make: long **i** (*like*) or short **i** (*in*)?_____

2. What does *counterfeit* mean? _____

3. Is counterfeit a good thing? Why or why not?_____

4. If you had three bills in your pocket and one-third of the paper money was fake, how many of the bills in your pocket are likely to be fake? _____

In the 1990s, new security features were added to several bills to prevent counterfeiting. Some of these features include color-shifting ink, microprinting, and a security thread. The first bill to be changed was the 100-dollar bill in 1991.

1. *Micro* is a prefix that means really tiny. What is *microprinting*?_____

2. What does *prevent* mean? _____

3. How many security features do we learn about in this paragraph? List them.

_____

4. Is counterfeiting a serious problem? _____

Paper Money

The Chinese were the first to use paper money. They began using paper money in the 600s. They also invented a way to print the money. It was about a thousand years later before Europeans began making paper money. The United States has had different types of paper money through the years.

Today, all the paper money in the United States is printed at the Bureau of Engraving and Printing in Washington, D.C.

Paper money is not actually made of paper. Paper would wear out too quickly. Paper money is made from cloth. You can see the threads if you hold a bill to the light. It's a blend of 25 percent cotton and 75 percent linen. This blend makes a strong bill, which lasts much longer than paper. Paper is made from wood pulp. It is much weaker than fabric. Special inks have to be carefully mixed to create the exact combination of colors for the paper money. There is a secret formula for this ink.

There are also special security threads in the bills. They are to prevent people from counterfeiting money. These threads were once made of metal, but now they're plastic or polyester. Before bills are sent out for use, they are pressed and starched. The starch makes them feel crispy.

1. Does the **ea** sound in *thread* sound more like the **ea** sound in **bread** or the **ea** sound in **bead**?

    _____

2. What is a synonym for *blend* as it is used in the article?
    a. separation
    b. combine
    c. mixture

3. What is a surprising fact about paper money? _____

    _____

    _____

4. Why is paper money made of cloth? _____

    _____

5. If the United States first issued paper money in 1775, about how much longer have the Chinese been using paper money?

    _____

    _____

Pirates and Money

Pirates robbed ships at sea. They stole what they considered valuable. Most often they stole gold and silver. A pirate stole for himself and his crew. Pirates were criminals.

1. What does the title tell us about the subject of this article? _____

2. What is a pirate's connection to money? _____

3. Is a pirate considered a "good guy"? Why or why not? _____
_____

4. Do pirates steal paper money? Why or why not? _____
_____

Privateers worked for governments. They were given permission to attack enemy ships during war. If a ship had treasure on board, privateers captured it. Privateers were not considered criminals.

1. What are the similarities between pirates and privateers? _____

2. Was taking treasure the main job of privateers? _____

3. When could privateers attack a ship? _____

4. What are the differences between pirates and privateers? _____
_____

In the 1500s, Spanish ships made many trips back and forth from Central and South America. They took silver and gold from the ancient native tribes called the Incas and Aztecs. They made coins from the gold and silver.

1. About how many years ago did the events in this paragraph take place? _____

2. Who stole silver and gold? _____

3. What did they make from the silver and gold? _____

4. Was it okay to take gold and sliver from the native tribes? Why or why not? _____
_____

Later, when the French and Spanish went to war, French privateers still attacked the Spanish ships. Pirates who attacked Spanish ships were known as buccaneers. Buccaneers stole the ships as well as their treasure. They built up their own fleet of ships. Some famous buccaneers were Red Legs Greaves, Rock Braziliano, and L'Olonnais the Terrible.

1. What are buccaneers? _____

2. What is the difference between privateers and buccaneers? _____

3. Which sentence gives names of some high-seas robbers? _____

4. Pick one name. How do you think that person got his name? _____

Day #1   *Day #2*   *Day #3*   *Day #4*

Assessment

1. Look at the title. How do you think this selection will be different from the earlier selection on pirates?

_____

Famous Pirates

Captain Kidd was a famous pirate. His real name was William Kidd. He was a seaman. He was hired to search for pirates. He worked as a privateer in England but began stealing for himself. He and his crew attacked the *Quedah Merchant*. They stole gold bars and coins worth about $93,000. They also stole the ship. Kidd was convicted of piracy and hanged in 1701. Some of his treasure was found in Long Island, New York. Some people believe there is more to be found.

2. How did Captain Kidd become a pirate?_____

_____

_____

Another famous pirate was Blackbeard. His real name was Edward Teach. He twisted his long black beard into long pigtails. In his belt he carried daggers, pistols, and a cutlass, which is a short, heavy sword with a curved blade. He terrified his enemies.

3. What made Blackbeard famous? _____

_____

_____

The British and American navies put a stop to most piracy at the end of the eighteenth century. However, there are still some pirates working today. Today's pirates have guns instead of swords.

4. Is being a pirate a safe lifestyle? Use clues from the entire article to help you answer that question.

_____

_____

_____

5. Which do you think is a more effective weapon for a pirate: a gun or a sword? Why?

_____

_____

_____

Ralph was a dirty mutt. His once-white hair was gray and brown with grime. He wore a black collar around his neck that had once been blue. On the dirty collar hung an identification tag, if anyone could get close enough to read it.

1. Circle the word that has a middle sound like *but*.
2. Circle a word the writer uses instead of *dirt*.
3. What is Ralph? _____
4. What details in the paragraph helped you decide this? _____

_____

Right now, Ralph was on his belly. He inched forward under the lilac bushes. His long hair dragged in the dirt. His bright, black eyes were glued on a plate at the edge of the table. On it was a ham sandwich. His moist, black nose twitched with the smell.

1. Circle the word that starts and ends with the same sound.
2. What does *moist* mean? _____
3. Is Ralph moving quickly or slowly? _____
4. Predict what will happen next. _____

I said, "It's time for bed." That announcement triggered a running marathon all through the house until I cornered Bart in the living room closet. I carried him up to his bedroom, and amazingly, he fell asleep almost immediately.

1. Circle the words with two or more letters that begin with a soft **a** sound.
2. Does the word *marathon* tell us that the writer chased Bart for a long time or a short time? _____
3. What was the effect on Bart of the writer's announcement that it was bedtime?

_____
4. Is the writer surprised that Bart fell asleep so quickly? _____

"The house looks great!" said Mrs. Bradford. "By the way, we would like to know if you can come back again tomorrow."

"Uh ... I don't think so, Mrs. Bradford. I'm pretty busy until next year—I mean next week."

While I lay in bed that night, I kept thinking that maybe someone had reversed a couple of letters in Bart's name.

1. If you undo the contraction *I'm*, what does it say? _____
2. What does *reversed* mean?_____
3. What word does the author think Bart's name should be? _____
4. What job do you think the writer has? _____

The Big Hill

When we first climbed into the car and strapped on our safety belts, I wasn't very nervous. I was sitting right next to my big brother and he had done this many times before. As we started to climb the hill, however, I could feel my heart jump into my throat.

"Brian?" I asked nervously. "Is this supposed to be so noisy?"

"Sure, Matthew," Brian answered. "It always does that."

A minute later we were going so fast down the hill I didn't have time to think. With a twist, a loop, and a bunch of fast turns, everyone on board screamed in delight. No wonder this was one of the most popular rides in the park. By the time the car pulled into the station and we got off the ride, I was ready to do it again!

1. Find the two contractions in this passage and undo them.

   _____

2. What is an antonym for *nervous*?

   _____

3. What effect did the ride have on Matthew as it started? What effect did it have at the end?

   _____

   _____

   _____

4. What are Matthew and Brian doing?

   _____

   _____

   _____

5. What clues from the passage helped you answer #4?

   _____

   _____

   _____

Two Friends, Two Problems

Dear Dennis,

Well, here I am at my aunt's house. How am I ever going to get everything she wants done? I only got to sit down for five minutes before she had me painting the stairs. She wants to wash the walls in the kitchen. She wants me to wax the floor in the hallway.

1. What does the title tell us about what will be in this story? _____
2. What does it sound like this friend's problem is? _____
3. How many separate tasks does this friend mention? _____
4. What are the tasks? _____

And did I tell you about the barn? She wants me to clean out all the old hay in the barn! It's got to be hundred-year-old hay! Every night I fall into bed, and then it feels like I get two minutes of sleep before it is morning again. I sure hope I survive and see you at school in September!

Ralph

1. What time of year is it?_____
2. What is the effect of the hard work on Ralph? _____
3. Do you think Ralph actually doubts that he'll survive the summer? _____
4. Think of a solution for Ralph's problem. _____

Dear Dennis,

Hey, I miss you! It is so quiet here at my grandmother's house. She doesn't own a TV! She must be the last person on the planet without one. All morning long, we sit and read, then we eat lunch, then we go for a little walk. After that, we read some more. The only time I get to see anyone is when we shop for groceries.

1. What is this friend's problem? _____
2. What is the first thing the author says in this letter?_____
3. Can you imagine spending the summer without television?_____
4. Do you think the author looks forward to going out for groceries? _____

Plus, Grandma won't let me help her with anything. If I offer to wash the dishes, she says, "No, dear, you are on vacation." If I offer to weed the garden, she says, "Oh, no, dear, I always do that." She even makes my bed! I hope I don't die of boredom before school starts!

Sheila

1. What new information do we find out about Sheila's problem? _____
2. Why do you think Ralph didn't write that he missed Dennis: because he doesn't like Dennis enough to miss him or because he doesn't have time to miss Dennis?

   _____
3. Compare Sheila's problem with Ralph's. _____
4. Which friend's problem would you rather have? Why? _____

1. Look at the title. Does it give you the idea that this reading will be funny or serious? Rewrite the title to give the opposite idea.

_____

Those Crazy Laws!

Wes watched the steam rise from the bowl of soup. He lifted the spoon to his mouth. SLURP!

"Wes, stop slurping your soup, or I'm calling the police," his sister Ada said.

2. How did Ada feel about her brother sipping soup? How do you know?

_____

Wes looked at Ada and laughed. "Go right ahead," he said. "They will think you are crazy."

"Sure the police will think I'm crazy, but they have to arrest you," responded Ada. "You are breaking a New Jersey law because you are not allowed to slurp soup in a public place."

"That's the craziest law I've ever heard!" he exclaimed.

"There are lots of crazy laws," said Ada. "New Jersey has another law that says people in Newark are not allowed to buy ice cream after 6:00 p.m. unless they have a note from a doctor. The one I like best is a law in Winnetka, Illinois, that says people cannot remove their shoes in a theater if their feet smell."

3. Which of the three crazy laws in the selection above do you think is the craziest? Why?

_____

_____

"How could cities have laws like that?" asked Wes.

"Many of these laws were passed over one hundred years ago. Life was totally different then," said Ada.

"Well, I don't want to get arrested," said Wes. "So I guess I'll eat my soup a little more quietly."

4. Why do some laws sound silly?

_____

5. Do you think police officers would make people obey a law today about buying ice cream? Explain.

_____

Does anyone like mosquitoes? Although the mosquito's high-pitched hum may be attractive to male mosquitoes, it signals danger to humans. When a mosquito "bites," it hurts, next it itches, and then we need to scratch.

1. Which words have a **ch** sound? _____

2. Circle an example of alliteration.

3. An *s* is added to the word *mosquito* in two different ways in this paragraph. What does each mean? _____

4. What sequence of events happens when a mosquito bites us? _____
   _____

We talk about mosquito "bites," but actually mosquitoes don't bite. They stab and sip their victim's blood. Only the female mosquito "bites" us since she needs blood for the development of the eggs inside her body.

1. What is *don't* a contraction of? _____

2. What word could we use instead of *actually*? _____

3. Is the writer trying to convince us to start calling mosquito bites mosquito stabs instead? _____

4. Why is it inaccurate to say that a mosquito bites? _____

Would you eat bugs? Many people know that bugs taste good and are good for you. In other parts of the world, eating insects is not unusual. Some insects have high nutritional value. Dried insects are 60 to 70 percent protein. Some insects are rich in lycine, an amino acid that helps muscles develop.

1. What words have a *c* with a soft **c** sound in the middle? _____

2. What other words could you use instead of "good" and "good for you" in the second sentence? _____

3. Do dried insects contain a little or a large amount of protein? _____

4. Did the writer of this paragraph write it to convince you to eat a bug today or to inform you about bugs being healthy to eat? _____

People eat insects not only because they are healthful but also because some insects taste great. Ant eggs cooked in butter are common in Mexico. Bolivians munch on a type of roasted ant as though they were peanuts. Crickets, caterpillars, termites, bees, and wasps also show up on menus around the world.

1. Find a word that begins and ends with the same sound. _____

2. Circle a word that the writer used instead of *eat*.

3. When a writer uses *as though*, is he or she comparing two things that are alike or contrasting two things that are different? _____

4. Name two reasons people eat insects. _____

Assessment

Some Insects Are Social Insects

Many animals live together in groups. They live together for different reasons. Some live together to find food, to raise their young, or to protect themselves from enemies. Animals that live together are like families or communities.

Most insects live alone. They find their own food, fight enemies by themselves, and raise babies alone.

Insects that live together are called social insects. They live in organized societies called colonies. Members of the colony have special jobs within the colony.

Because they live and work together, termites are social insects. Their nests are mounds of dirt. Inside the mounds are tunnels and rooms. Termites live in warm places. They feed off wood. The largest termites are the queens, which lay eggs every day. Some queens live for 50 years. Worker termites are small. They gather food and build nests. Soldier termites, which have large, strong heads, guard the nest. People don't like termites because termites eat the wood in a house. When people find out their home has termites, they generally call an exterminator.

If social insects lived alone, they would die. A social insect can survive only as part of its society.

1. Three words have a *c* in the middle; each has a different sound. Which word has a middle *c* with a **sh** sound? Which word has a middle *c* with a hard **c** sound? Which word has a middle *c* with a soft **c** sound?

   _____

2. What other word could you use instead of *exterminate*?

   a. increase

   b. remove

   c. tolerate

3. Which termite has the most jobs? What are they? _____

   _____

4. Why did the author write this passage?

   a. to convince us that social insects are better than insects who live alone

   b. to gross us out with the image of wood-eating insects

   c. to inform us about the lives and habits of social insects

5. How are ants similar to the social insects mentioned in the article?

   _____

   _____

   _____

Insects in Winter

In the summertime, insects can be seen buzzing and fluttering around us. But as winter's cold weather begins, the insects seem to disappear. Do you know where they go?

1. What does the title tell us about the topic of this article? _____

2. How do the opening sentences narrow down the topic you guessed from the title? _____

3. Where do you think insects go during winter? _____

4. What two seasons are not compared in the first paragraph? _____

Day #1

Many insects find a warm place to spend the winter.

Ants try to dig deep into the ground. Some beetles stack up in piles under rocks or dead leaves. Honeybees gather in a ball in the middle of their hive. The bees stay in this tight ball trying to stay warm.

1. Which sentence answers the question from Day #1? _____

2. Which animals are listed as examples? _____

3. What shapes do the insects form while trying to stay warm? _____

4. Which insect goes underground? _____

Day #2

Female grasshoppers don't even stay around for winter. In the fall, they lay their eggs and die. The eggs hatch in the spring.

1. Which insect does not live through the winter?_____

2. What is her survival tactic? _____

3. Does this paragraph tell you why the eggs of the grasshopper are able to survive the winter but the adults are not? _____

4. How long do female grasshoppers live? _____

Day #3

Winter is very hard for insects, but each spring the survivors come out, and the buzzing and fluttering begins again.

1. Does every type of insect survive the winter? _____

2. Do you think ants in Florida have to dig deep in the ground to survive winter? Why or why not? _____

3. Given your answer to #2, what part of the country does this article describe?

_____

4. Which insects mentioned in this article do not buzz or flutter? _____

Day #4

1. What question will this article answer?

_____

How a Mosquito Bites

The mosquito has a long, tube-like proboscis. This is the mosquito's mouth. The proboscis stabs a victim and then acts like a straw. A female mosquito may drink the blood of humans, frogs, birds, or other animals. A male will sip from plants. Liquids are the mosquito's only diet.

2. Will a male mosquito drink your blood?

_____

When the mosquito "bites," it stabs through the victim's skin with six needle-like stylets, which form the center of the proboscis. The stylets poke into the skin and then bend to enter a blood vessel. While the mosquito is sucking the blood, it leaves saliva under the person's skin. Most of us are allergic to this saliva. That's what makes us itch.

3. What parts of a mosquito are involved in drinking blood?

_____

_____

Mosquitoes also spread harmful diseases. Certain mosquitoes carry the germs that cause diseases such as malaria and yellow fever. They leave germs when they "bite." Many of the mosquitoes that spread diseases live in hot, moist lands near the equator. But the mosquitoes are found in all parts of the world—even the Arctic.

4. List two unpleasant effects of a mosquito bite.

_____

_____

5. Is reading this article making you itch anywhere? If so, guess why.

_____

_____

_____

_____

A chameleon is a reptile. Like all reptiles, it has scaly skin. A chameleon has two interesting body parts. It has a long, sticky tongue. When the chameleon sees an insect, its tongue can fly out and back in less than a second. A chameleon can also change the color of its skin. The color of the skin helps it hide from enemies.

1. What sound does *chameleon* start with: **ch** like **chart** or hard **c** like **cart**?_____

2. What is a chameleon?_____

3. What are its two interesting body parts? _____

4. Is it helpful or just cool that a chameleon can change its skin color? _____
   Give a detail from the story to support your answer._____

Day #1

When my reptile hatches, I'll be so proud!
Its baby cry will be so loud.
We'll go walking, it will look distinct,
Towering above me—it's NOT extinct!

1. Is the **a** sound in *hatches* the same as the **a** sound in *watches*?_____

2. What happens when an animal hatches? _____

3. Will the baby reptile be larger or smaller than the author? _____

4. Circle the clues in the poem that helped you answer #3.

Day #2

Salvador Dali painted in an unusual style. The items you could see in Dali's works were things you might see every day, but Dali changed them. He made them look unusual. For example, one of his paintings shows clocks that are melting.

1. *Un* is a prefix that means "not." What does *unusual* mean?_____

2. What other words could you use instead of *unusual*?_____

3. What detail tells you about Dali's painting style? _____

4. Why did the writer write the paragraph?

   a. to entertain   b. to inform   c. to give an opinion

Day #3

The spaceship had been traveling through space for two hundred years. The people on board were just coming out of stasis. They hadn't been awake since 2020. The computer was set to wake them up when the planet X59 was a week's travel away.

1. Circle the compound word.

2. What does it mean to be in stasis? _____

3. What clues from the paragraph helped you answer #2?_____

   _____

4. How far away is planet X59? _____

Day #4

Blue or Red?

Assessment

Lord Kent and his family sat on benches in the main room of the castle. The evening supper was cleared away, and the family was enjoying the songs and stories of Odo.

Odo was a minstrel who traveled from castle to castle to entertain the people along the way. He would sing songs, play instruments, tell stories, and do simple tricks. In return, the people fed Odo and let him sleep in the castle.

Odo picked up a sack and dumped out some red and blue balls. Lord Kent's youngest son, William, ran after the balls and gathered them in his hands. The little boy carefully handed them back to the minstrel.

"Thank you kindly for your help, Master William," said Odo. "Will you stay and help me with this next trick, too?" The young boy smiled and nodded his head up and down.

"How many balls do you see?" asked Odo.

"There are six balls in all," answered William.

"And how many blue balls do you see?" asked Odo.

"There are four blue balls," said the boy.

"I am going to put all of the balls back in the sack," announced Odo. "Then, I will ask you to select one ball. I will make a prediction about the color of the ball you will choose each time. I think the first ball will be blue."

William reached into the sack, and sure enough, he pulled out a blue ball!

1. Find a word from the first two paragraphs that has a silent consonant in the middle of the word.

   _____

2. What is a minstrel? _____

3. Why did the author write this selection?

   a. to inform us about the difficulties of being a minstrel
   b. to entertain us with a fun story
   c. to tell us how to predict the color of the ball coming out of the sack

4. What was the probability that William would choose a blue ball from the sack the first time? Write your answer as a fraction.

   _____

5. Why was Odo's prediction a good one?

   _____

   _____

John Glenn

On November 5, 1998, Senator John Glenn traveled into space as the oldest astronaut ever. He was seventy-seven years old.

1. What does the title tell us about the subject of this article? _____

2. How do the opening sentences narrow the focus of the article?

    _____

3. Do you know any people who are around seventy-seven years old? _____

4. Can you imagine them traveling into space? Why or why not? _____

    _____

Day #1

Years earlier, John Glenn was the first American to circle Earth. During that trip in 1962, he traveled on the *Friendship 7*. He was the only person on board. That space ship had no computers and only one window. Scientists wanted to observe Glenn's reaction to the space environment.

1. What new information about John Glenn and space did you find out?

    _____

2. What details does this paragraph tell you about that first space flight?

    _____

3. Does the paragraph tell you how high up *Friendship 7* was? _____

4. How is the space environment different from the earth environment? _____

Day #2

In 1998, John Glenn went into space on the space shuttle *Discovery*. This time, there were six other astronauts on board. They had ten windows and five computers. This time, scientists wanted to observe the reaction of an older man in the space environment.

1. What do the two flights have in common? _____

2. How are the two flights different? You may want to make a chart. _____

3. What kind of space vehicle is *Discovery*? _____

4. Which trip sounds more fun? Why? _____

Day #3

Glenn was an American hero in 1962 for orbiting the earth. John Glenn became a hero again in 1998 when he traveled as the oldest astronaut to orbit the earth.

1. How many years passed between Glenn's first and second flights? _____

2. How old were you in 1998? _____

3. Was your teacher alive in 1962? _____
    If so, does your teacher remember that space flight? _____

4. Do you agree with the author's opinion that John Glenn is an American hero?
    Why or why not? _____

    _____

Day #4

Assessment

1. Look over the writing below. What kind of writing is this?

    a. a children's story

    b. a newspaper article

    c. a poem

Men Land on the Moon

By Jane Smith

City News Staff Writer

HOUSTON—On July 20, 1969, two Americans made history. Astronauts Neil Armstrong and Edwin "Buzz" Aldrin landed on the moon. They were the first men to walk on the moon. NASA officials waited anxiously to hear a message. The message was, "The *Eagle* has landed." The *Eagle* was their landing craft. Michael Collins stayed in the command module. He orbited the moon while waiting for Armstrong and Aldrin.

2. How many astronauts went into space in July 1969?_____

The Apollo 11 spacecraft left Earth on July 16, 1969. The rocket lifted off from Cape Canaveral, Florida. This was not the first manned trip to the moon. Apollo 8 was the first in 1968.

Americans watched the first moon walk on television. Armstrong climbed down the *Eagle's* ladder. He stepped onto the moon's surface. He said, "That's one small step for man, one giant leap for mankind." People around the world heard these words.

3. How many days were there between lift-off and the astronaut's moon walk?

    _____

The astronauts wore spacesuits. These suits protected them from getting too hot or too cold. Sturdy plastic helmets protected their heads. Visors protected their eyes against the sun's rays. They wore moon boots to protect their feet on the rocky surface. Gloves protected their hands. Their underwear had a built-in cooling system. They carried portable life-support systems on their backs. They needed them because there is no air on the moon. Their suits had built-in radios, so they could talk to each other and with NASA. A television camera transmitted pictures to Earth.

4. Armstrong says, "That's one small step for man, one giant leap for mankind." If he's talking about himself stepping off the ladder in the "small step" part, what is he talking about in the "giant leap" part?

    _____

5. Reread the last paragraph. Do you think the people seeing the moon landing on television could see any of Neil Armstrong's skin?

    _____

Cotton grows in hot climates. It requires a long growing season. The plants need plenty of sunshine and water. Some cotton fields are irrigated. Cotton plants are related to okra and hibiscus plants. They are also hot-weather plants.

1. What word sounds like the phrase *caught on*? _____

2. What does *irrigated* mean? _____

3. What is the main idea of this paragraph?
   - a. Cotton is easy to grow.   b. Cotton is a hot-weather plant.
   - c. Cotton is grown in all parts of the U.S.

4. Where is cotton more likely to be grown: **Maine** or **Mississippi**?_____

The cotton plant produces white, fluffy balls of fiber. These fibers are very strong. Therefore, cloth made from cotton fibers is also strong. Cotton fibers are very absorbent. Because of that they are easy to dye. Fabrics made from cotton may be easily dyed many different colors.

1. Name two words that rhyme with *cloth*. _____

2. What word sounds like *dye* but means to stop living?_____

3. What is the main idea of this paragraph? _____

4. What makes cotton a good fabric? _____

Cottonseeds were once thrown away as waste. Now cottonseed oil is used in many foods and in soaps and cosmetics. The hulls are used to feed cattle. Parts of the seeds are used for padding in furniture and cars.

1. Circle all the words with three syllables.

2. What is waste? _____

3. What is the main idea of the above passage?
   - a. Cottonseeds are waste.   b. Cottonseeds have many uses.
   - c. Cows eat the hulls of cottonseeds.

4. Are cottonseeds edible? _____

The jeans you may be wearing are probably made of cotton. Your T-shirts are made of cotton. The doughnuts you had as an after-school snack might have been made with cottonseed oil. The sheets on your bed may be made of cotton.

1. Do you pronounce the **gh** in *doughnuts*? _____

2. What other word could you use instead of *probably*? _____

3. What is the main idea of this paragraph?_____

4. One of the examples is not like the others. Which one is the odd example?

_____

Slaves and the Crop-Over Festival

Slaves were brought to the islands in the Caribbean Sea in the 1600s. About 10 million slaves ended up in the area. The slaves were brought over to work on the sugarcane plantations. Slaves planted, cared for, and then harvested the sugarcane.

Sugarcane is a plant that has jointed stems. Sugar is found in the stems. Most sugarcane in the world is still harvested by hand.

After slaves cut the cane, they had to make it into sugar within two days or else the cane would spoil. The slaves had to work quickly. They squeezed the juice from the stems in a pressing machine. Then they boiled the juice in a big pot until it formed thick syrup. Sugar crystals formed at the bottom of the pot. Slaves put the sugar crystals in one keg. They put the juice in another. Then they took the kegs to awaiting ships. The sugar was sold in the United States and Europe. After the cane was loaded onto the ship, a slave shouted, "Crop-over!" and the celebration began. They celebrated the harvest by dancing and feasting.

This festival is still celebrated on the island of Barbados. It lasts for three weeks. There is a parade. People sell arts and crafts. Islanders make straw mats, wooden sculptures, and clay pottery. At the end of the festival, there is a band contest and fireworks.

1. Fill in the blank with a word that is spelled differently but sounds like *band*.
   Slaves were _____ from making money for themselves from the sugarcane harvest.

2. What is a plantation? _____
   _____

3. Fill in the blanks with the word *before* or *after*.

   a. Slaves boiled the juice _____ putting it in kegs.

   b. A slave called "Crop-over" _____ the sugarcane was loaded on the ship.

   c. Slaves squeezed the juice from sugarcane _____ they cut the canes.

4. What is the main topic of paragraph 3? _____
   _____
   _____

5. How is the original festival different from the festival celebrated now in Barbados?
   _____
   _____
   _____

Mold

Perhaps you have seen a green, fuzzy spot on bread or cheese. If so, it was probably mold.

1. What does the title tell you about the subject of this article?_____

2. Have you ever seen green, fuzzy spots on bread or cheese? _____

3. What would you do if you saw a green, fuzzy spot on a piece of cheese you were about to eat?_____

4. Do you guess that this will be an informative article or an entertaining story?

_____

Day #1

Mold is a kind of plant called fungi. The most common molds are green or black. Mold likes to grow in a moist, warm place. But where does it come from?

Mold comes from spores, which exist in the air. If these spores find a moist, warm place, they will produce mold. Mold grows in webs of fuzzy branches. It continues to grow as long as the conditions are right.

1. What is mold? _____

2. Where does mold come from? _____

3. Where does mold like to grow? _____

4. What image does the author use to describe how mold grows? _____

Day #2

Foods, such as cheese, fruit, and bread, can develop mold if they are left out in a warm, damp room. Mold may even grow on leather shoes, belts, or furniture.

1. Did this paragraph tell you what mold will grow on?_____

2. If so, what?_____

3. How many categories are the examples grouped in? _____

4. What are the categories?_____

_____

Day #3

Mold is usually thought of as a problem. But some molds are valuable to scientists. The most famous mold is called *penicillium notatum*. This mold is used to make a valuable drug called penicillin.

1. What new information did you find out about mold?_____

2. What specific mold is mentioned?_____

3. Can you imagine being grateful for mold? _____

4. Have you ever had a bacterial infection like an ear infection? _____
   If so, there's a good chance you took medicine that was derived from penicillin—you took mold!

Day #4

1. Do flowers need to tell time? What else might the title mean?

_____

The Flower Clock

Have you ever seen a clock made of flowers? A Swedish man, Carl Linnaeus, made one. He was a botanist. Botanists study plants. Linnaeus lived in the eighteenth century. He grew a flower clock called "The Garden of Hours." He planted a circle of flowers. The circle represented a clock. Flowers grew at the 12:00 position. They grew at the 1:00 position. Flowers grew at each hour.

2. Name any year in the eighteenth century. _____

Linnaeus called the flower clock his "Watch of Flora." *Flora* means plants. His watch had 46 flowers. Each flower opened and closed at different hours. Flowers respond to light and dark. He designed the flower clock to work in Sweden. It works at latitude 60° north. It wouldn't work in the United States.

3. What is a flower clock, and how can you tell time with it?

_____

_____

Here is a list of flowers and the times they open or close in the United States. You might want to grow your own flower clock.

2:00 a.m.   Moonflowers close.
5:00 a.m.   Morning glories open.
9:00 a.m.   Tulips open and water lilies close.
10:00 a.m. California poppies open.
12:00 noon Chicory closes.
4:00 p.m.   Four o'clocks open.
5:00 p.m.   Evening primroses open.
7:00 p.m.   Iceland poppies close.
9:00 p.m.   Moonflowers open.
10:00 p.m. Queen-of-the-Night opens.

4. List all the flowers that have a name that makes sense for the time they open.

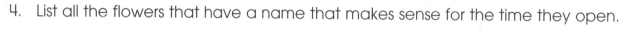
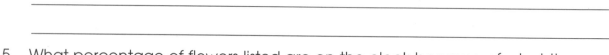

_____

_____

_____

5. What percentage of flowers listed are on the clock because of what time they open?

_____

Lacy kicked the leaves in her yard. She didn't want to help her dad rake. She had made plans to go skating at the rink with her friends. "I just need a little help this morning, Lacy," said her dad. "You can spend the rest of the afternoon with your friends."

Lacy didn't say anything as she set to work, rhythmically moving the rake back and forth.

"Have you ever studied these leaves?" her dad asked. "It amazes me that so many of them are symmetrical."

1. Which word has both a short **a** and long **a** in it? _____
2. Is moving rhythmically moving **steadily** or **unevenly**? _____
3. What season is described above? _____
4. What clues helped you answer #3? _____

Day #1

"Look at this sweet gum leaf," he said. "When you fold the leaf in half along the length of its stem, it looks the same on each side, including the veins. Something is symmetrical when there is a mirror image. The center fold line is the line of symmetry."

1. Which word has the same **ei** sound as in *veins*: **height** or **reign**? _____
2. What does *symmetrical* mean? _____
3. How do you find the line of symmetry? _____
4. What is the line of symmetry? _____

_____

Day #2

Jailee and her dad bent over the table drawing the plans for the tree house. "So, what do you think, Jailee?" he asked. "Is this the size you had in mind? Are there enough windows?"

"It seems so small," Jailee answered.

"It's bigger than you think," her dad said. "This drawing is just a scale model."

1. Circle the words that sound like *sew*.
2. Put a line through the sentence where *drawing* means *a picture*.
3. How does Jailee feel about the drawing? _____
4. Whose idea was it to build a tree house? _____

Day #3

"A scale model is a drawing that has the same proportions, or sizes, as the true widths and lengths of a structure. The drawing reduces the actual size, but the proportions are the same. Look at the bottom of the page where you see 1 cm = 1 m."

1. Which meaning of *scale* does the author use here?
   a. a fish scale   b. an instrument to weigh things
   c. something that shows the relationship between a drawing and an actual item
2. Does *reduces* mean **makes bigger** or **makes smaller**? _____
3. What is the same in both a scale drawing and the true size of a structure?

_____

4. Why is it important to have a scale on a drawing? _____

Day #4

The Kite-Eating Tree

"Another kite eaten by the tree," Manny muttered.

"My dad has a 24-foot ladder. If we knew how tall the tree was, we might be able to use it to get the kite," said Kate.

"Hey, that's a great idea!" shouted Manny. "Let's find out how tall this tree is. We did something like this in math class. We measured a stick and its shadow, and then we measured the shadow of a tree. We used equivalent fractions to calculate the height of a tree."

"That's right!" exclaimed Kate. "You go get a tape measure, and I'll find a short tree. We can measure a little tree and its shadow the same way we measured the stick."

When Manny came back, he had a tape measure, some paper, and a pencil. Kate stood beside a short pine tree. The two friends quickly set to work. They found that the height of the short tree was 4 feet tall. Its shadow was 6 feet tall. When Manny and Kate measured the shadow of the tree holding the kite, they found that its shadow was 30 feet long.

Manny quickly wrote an equation with fractions using the measurements from the trees. After Manny worked the problem, he yelled, "The tree is 20 feet tall! Your dad's ladder will reach up that high!"

1. Which words in this story start the same as *equal*?

   _____

2. What is a shadow?

   _____

   _____

3. How do you mutter?

   _____

   _____

4. What did Kate do while Manny went to get the tape measure?

   _____

   _____

   _____

5. Where do you think Manny and Kate will fly the kite next time?

   _____

   _____

   _____

Marie Curie

One of the greatest scientists of all time is Marie Curie.

Day #1

1. What does the title tell you about the subject of this article?_____
2. What new information does this sentence give you? _____
3. Is this sentence a fact or the opinion of the author? _____
4. Have you heard of Marie Curie? _____

Marie Curie was born in Poland in 1867. She studied at a university in Paris and lived in France for most of her adult life. Along with her husband, Pierre Curie, she studied radioactivity. She was awarded the Nobel Prize in chemistry in 1911 for her work discovering radium and polonium.

Day #2

1. What details do you learn about her personal life in this paragraph?_____
2. What details do you learn about her professional life as a scientist? _____
3. Have you heard of the Nobel Prize before? _____
4. Does it sound like a big deal to win it? _____

The discovery of radium was a turning point in history. Some medical advances based on the research of the Curies are the X-ray and the use of radiation to treat cancer.

Day #3

1. What benefits of Marie's work are discussed here? _____
2. Does this paragraph say that Marie invented the X-ray?_____
3. What is a *turning point in history*: something that changes life for everyone or something that changes life for only a few people?
_____
4. Do you know anyone who is a cancer survivor?_____
If so, you can thank Marie Curie, in part, for that person's survival.

The Curies were both generous people. Even though they were poor for most of their lives, they did not patent any of their discoveries so that everyone could benefit from their research. Marie Curie died in 1934. The world should not forget her.

Day #4

1. Is the last sentence a fact or the author's opinion?_____
2. Find a sentence in any part of the article that is a fact._____
3. If you were a scientist, do you think you would patent your research? Why or why not?_____
4. Do you agree that Marie Curie probably is one of the greatest scientists of all time? Why or why not? _____

Assessment

1. Have you ever heard of Philo Farnsworth?

_____

Philo Farnsworth and Television

What would you say if someone asked who had invented the transmission, or sending, of television images? If you do not know the answer, you are not alone. Most people do not know that this was an idea of Philo Farnsworth. This is probably because a large company took Farnsworth's idea.

2. Why have most people not heard of Philo Farnsworth?

_____

_____

_____

_____

Farnsworth was born in a log cabin in 1906. When he was twelve, his family moved to a ranch. This put Farnsworth miles away from his school, and he rode his horse to get there.

Farnsworth was very interested in the electron and electricity. He asked one of his teachers to teach him outside of class and to let him sit in on a course for older students. The teacher agreed. He had the idea for sending television pictures when he was only fourteen.

3. What year did Farnsworth have the idea? _____

An article told of his invention when he was only twenty-two. How did it work? Moving images, or pictures, were broken into pinpoints of light. These pinpoints were changed into electrical impulses, or movements. Then the impulses were collected by the television set and changed back to light. People could see the images. A major magazine listed Farnsworth as one of the 100 great scientists and thinkers of the twentieth century.

4. What year did the article appear? _____

5. Which scientist do you think is greater: Marie Curie or Philo Farnsworth? Why?

_____

_____

_____

_____

_____

I thought the bottom of the ocean was exactly like the part near the shore, the part I waded into. I thought it was smooth and flat with lots of sand. Many years later, I was surprised to find out that wasn't true at all. There are hills and mountains down there. There are plains and valleys and trenches.

1. What are the two words in the contraction *wasn't*? _____

2. What does *exactly* mean? _____

3. How are the bottom of the ocean and the earth's surface similar? _____

4. How are they different? _____

Mermaids are creatures whose head and upper body are a beautiful woman. The lower body is a fish. Mermaids tend to fall in love with humans. They may try to lure sailors into the ocean with them.

1. Does the *ea* in *creatures* sound like the *ea* in **create** or **features**? _____

2. Does *lure* mean **attract** or **warn**? _____

3. Circle the words that tell us whether mermaids always do the things in this paragraph.

4. Does a mermaid sound like a **real** or an **imaginary** creature? _____

Some people say mermaids can predict the future. Others say mermaids have supernatural powers. Legends tell of mermaids' castles under the sea. The word *mermaid* comes from the Latin word *mare*. *Mare* means "sea" or "lake."

1. *Super* is a prefix that means "over" or "above." So what does *supernatural* mean? _____

2. What does the paragraph say *mare* means? _____

3. If *mare* becomes *mer* over time, what does *mermaid* mean as a compound word? _____

4. Do all people believe in mermaids? _____

Wood carvers designed, carved, and painted figureheads for ships. Figureheads made each ship unique. They are fixed to the prow of a ship. The prow is the front. Figureheads often depicted mermaids.

1. What word in the paragraph is a compound of two other words? _____

2. What is a figurehead? _____

3. What is the main subject of this paragraph, mermaids or figureheads?

_____

4. How do figureheads make each ship unique? _____

Day #1

Day #2

Day #3

Day #4

Assessment

The Music of the Humpbacks

Humpback whales sing. Sailors have heard their music for thousands of years. In the 1950s, the U.S. Navy first recorded their sounds. Each sound the whale makes is called a unit. A whale may sing the unit once or may repeat it several times in a row. Often a series of three or four different units is sung in a specific order called a phrase. Humpbacks repeat phrases several times to make a theme. The sounds are organized in ways that make them songs. An average whale song lasts about 12 minutes, and it may have three to five themes. Humpbacks sing their songs over and over again for hours, but only males sing. Singing is part of their courting ritual, and they sing only in breeding season. Songs of the North Atlantic humpback are different from those of the North Pacific humpbacks.

When they sing, whales hang their heads down in about 60 feet (18 m) of water. They move their flippers slowly to stay in the same position.

Researchers use underwater equipment to record the songs, but the songs can be heard without using the equipment. Songs can travel 4 to 5 miles (6 to 8 km) underwater. Female whales can hear the songs from far away.

1. Fill in the blank with a word that is a homophone of *whale*. The whale sings, it doesn't just _____.

2. What word in paragraph 1 means to do something over and over again?

   _____

3. Does the compound word in the name of the humpback whale give you a clue about what it looks like? What does it look like?

   _____

4. Name the three parts of a whale song, in order from smallest to largest.

   _____

   _____

   _____

   _____

5. Can the whale chew gum and walk at the same time (that is, can it sing and swim at the same time)? Which clue from the article helped you answer that question?

   _____

   _____

   _____

Name

The Incredible George Washington Carver

George Washington Carver was born in 1861. His parents were slaves. They lived on a plantation in Missouri.

1. What does the title tell us about the subject of this article? _____

2. What opinion word is in the title? _____

3. Was George born into a privileged situation? _____

4. Who was he named after? _____

Day #1

George Washington Carver was often sick as a child. He couldn't help around the plantation. He liked to spend time in the woods. There he found and studied flowers and plants. George taught himself to read. He left the plantation to live on his own when he was ten years old.

1. What was the effect of George's childhood illnesses? _____

2. What did George do instead of work in the plantation? _____

3. What is a surprising fact in the end of the paragraph? _____

4. Can you imagine leaving home and living on your own in the next year or so?
_____

Day #2

George wanted to go to a college. The college refused to admit him because he was black. George Washington Carver finally went to college and was an excellent student. He took botany and chemistry classes. After he graduated, he taught classes at a college in Iowa. He was also director of a greenhouse.

1. Does George give up easily? _____

2. What clues helped you answer #1? _____

3. What kind of classes are botany and chemistry: **literature** or **science**? _____

4. What details tell you whether Carver was a hard worker? _____
_____

Day #3

George Washington Carver was a scientist. He discovered over three hundred uses for the peanut plant. Among his discoveries were shampoo, car grease, soap, rubber, wood filler, paint, and shoe polish. His research helped farmers.

1. What was the effect of George's research? _____

2. What character traits did George have? _____

3. What was the effect of George's plant collecting when he was a boy?
_____

4. Do you agree that George Washington Carver is incredible? Why or why not?

Day #4

1. Do you think the name in the title is of a man whose first name is Duke? Or do you think it is about a man who is an English nobleman?

_____

Duke Ellington

When people hear Duke Ellington's name, they often think of "jazz." When he was a child, he took piano lessons. But he wasn't excited about playing the piano. Instead, he wanted to be on the baseball field.

2. What is the conflict in the above paragraph?

_____

_____

_____

As Ellington grew older, he heard more and more piano players. He heard music in many styles. By the time he was in high school, he had developed a true love for the piano and had written his first piece of music. He began to play the piano at parties. He also played at clubs and dances. Ellington eventually had his own musical group.

3. How was the conflict resolved?

_____

_____

_____

Ellington decided to move to New York. He played in the famous Cotton Club. Soon, his music was broadcast over the radio. He was on the road to stardom. He quickly became one of the biggest names in jazz.

4. Did Ellington listen only to jazz? _____

5. Which of the following is **not** a lesson you can take away from this story?

   a. Don't quit an activity right away.

   b. You can make a living doing what you love.

   c. The piano is better than baseball.

My scout troop just completed the best trip ever! We spent the day rafting down a river. When we first entered the water, it was so calm and clear that we could see the rocks two feet down. I thought the trip was going to be very boring because we moved so slowly. Was I wrong!

1. Circle all the words that sound like *too*.

2. What word could you use instead of *completed*?_____

3. What did they float on while they went down the river? _____

4. Was the author excited about the scout trip? _____

Within an hour, we had paddled to the main part of the river where the water rushed swiftly against the banks. The river wasn't very wide, and there were so many rapids that I thought we would crash into some of the rocks in the middle of the river, but we didn't. Some water and rocks ended up in the raft, though. I was amazed to see small bits of rock and dirt from water that looked so clear!

1. Which words that end in *-ed* have only one syllable?_____

2. What are rapids: **swift-moving** or **slow-moving** water? _____

3. List all the ways the author describes the river. _____

4. What was in the water that surprised the author? _____

Our river guide, Sue, said that the force of the water eroded the dirt from the riverbanks and broke off small bits of rocks. She said that most of the sediment washed downstream and greatly changed the land and water near the end of the river.

1. List all the compound words in this paragraph._____

2. Does *eroded* mean **added to** or **broke off**? _____

3. What is the effect of the water rushing against the riverbanks? _____

   _____

4. What is sediment? _____

Some of the soil and rock fell to the bottom of the river. The sediment made small islands and built new riverbanks. When the river flooded, the soil and rock flowed over the banks and across the land. The sediment left behind made the soil rich in nutrients for growing crops.

1. What word has a silent *s*? _____

2. Are *nutrients* **food** or **plants**? _____

3. List one effect of sediment falling to the bottom of the river. _____

4. What does the paragraph tell us might be good about the river flooding?

   _____

The Ice Hotel

How would you like to sleep in a room made of ice? Do you think it would be fun to sleep on a bed made of ice, too? Maybe you would like to drink from a glass made of ice? In Canada, you can try each of these things!

From the beginning of January to the end of March, the Ice Hotel is open for business. The building is made only from ice and snow. The building and the furniture are all made of ice. You will probably want to wear a coat inside. The whole building is a chilly 25°F.

People enjoy visiting this hotel. There is so much to see and do. The hotel has a place to watch movies. There are even two art galleries. Can you guess what kind of art you will see? You guessed it—ice sculptures!

When the winter season ends, the sun warms the building and it begins to melt. The solid ice turns back into liquid, and as the sun shines, the water evaporates. The Ice Hotel is gone, but only for a while. The cold winter winds will blow again. The evaporated water will collect into clouds. The clouds will get heavy with rain. And the rain will fall...as snow and ice!

1. List all the words with three syllables.

   _____

2. What does *evaporate* mean?

   a. to turn into vapor

   b. to seep into the ground

   c. to refreeze

3. Are you one of the people who would enjoy visiting this hotel? Why or why not?

   _____

   _____

   _____

4. What is the effect of warm sunshine on the Ice Hotel each year?

   _____

   _____

   _____

5. How does the Ice Hotel come back as snow and ice?

   _____

   _____

   _____

Letter to Grandma

Dear Grandma,

I am glad that you are having a good time on the beach. I'll bet it is warm there. I can't wait to get there during spring vacation. I want to go fishing with you and Grandpa and pick up shells on the beach.

1. What does the title tell us this piece is going to be? _____
2. Is the author writing in response to a letter from Grandma? _____
   If so, which sentence gives you that idea? _____
3. What season do you think it is? _____
4. What clues helped you answer #3? _____

Day #1

It is snowing like crazy here. Don't tell my mom I told you, but Mom cracked up the car yesterday. Some guy crashed right into the back of the car. It was just too icy. Mom was really upset. She even "cooked" at a restaurant on the way home. I hope she will pick up take-out food more often, even when the car is OK.

1. How is Grandma's climate different from the author's climate? _____
2. What effect did the snow have? _____
3. What was the effect of the car accident on the author's mother? _____
   _____
4. Does the author sound happy or unhappy about eating take-out? _____

Day #2

I had fun in the snow. We have a huge sledding hill. Meg and I went down it over and over. We made a family of snowmen, too. Then we got cold. My fingers and toes felt like they were going to fall right off! My snow pants were soaked through, and my nose and cheeks were redder than all get out.

1. Was the snow all bad for the author's family? _____
2. What was fun about the snow? _____
3. What was the effect of all the fun in the snow? _____
   _____
4. Did the author's fingers and toes actually fall off? _____

Day #3

Hey, is your nose red? Are you wearing sunscreen? I sure miss you. I'll see you soon.

                                     Love,
                                     Ian

1. Why might Grandma's nose be red? _____
2. Why does Ian ask her about wearing sunscreen? _____
3. Does Ian love his grandma? _____
4. What clues from the entire letter helped you answer #3? _____
   _____

Day #4

1. What is the greatest gift you've ever been given?

_____

_____

The Greatest Gift

When Rena walked in the door at home, her little brother grabbed her by the arm. "Rena, Rena, will you make a picture for Grandpa's birthday? I wrote a poem for him, but I want to put it with a great big picture. And I want you to do it because you're such a great artist."

Rena smiled. "Okay, Oscar. Grab all those old pictures from the box."

2. What did the first two paragraphs tell us about the three characters in this story?

_____

_____

_____

Oscar skipped out of the room. A few minutes later, he dashed in, carrying Grandpa's photos. It was hard to piece them together because they were all torn, and they were faded, too.

At the art studio, Rena laid the torn and faded photos across a table so she could arrange them in a special way. For weeks, Rena worked with her paints on a big canvas. She placed every stroke and chose every color with great care.

3. What kind of art does Rena do?

_____

On Grandpa's birthday, Oscar read his poem. Then Rena gave Grandpa the painting. Tears filled Grandpa's eyes. "The poem was wonderful, and the painting... the painting shows my old friends and my old neighborhood in a way that makes me feel as though I'm there all over again. Rena, you've shown me how special all these people have been in my life. You and Oscar are wonderful."

4. What is the time frame of the story?

_____

_____

5. Why did Grandpa cry after he saw the painting?

_____

_____

Abebe Bikila ran the marathon in Rome. He was the first person to run barefoot. He had practiced running that way many times. He had run the marathon only two other times. He won the race. Four years later he won in Tokyo. He finished that race in 2 hours, 12 minutes, and 11.2 seconds. He was the first person to win two consecutive races.

1. What word in the paragraph sounds like *one*? _____
2. What is the opposite of *barefoot*? _____
3. What units of time are mentioned in the paragraph? _____
4. What does *consecutive* mean? a. very long b. very hard c. following in order

Day #1

In the 1936 Olympics in Berlin, Germany, Jessie Owens set an Olympic record for the long jump. The record was 26 feet, 5 ½ inches. He won four gold medals. He also won the 100 meters, 200 meters, and 4 x 100 relay. Nazi Germany was a racist government. Jessie Owens was an African American.

1. Circle the word that has two different vowels that have the same sound.
2. What does *racist* mean?
   a. harmful   b. believing some races are better than others   c. war-loving
3. What is a big idea in this paragraph? _____
4. The Nazi government was happy that Jesse Owens won four gold medals at the 1936 Olympics. Is that statement **true** or **false**? _____

Day #2

Jackie Joyner-Kersee entered the heptathlon in Seoul. She won the 100-meter hurdles. She led in the high jump. She did well in the shot put and won the 200-meter dash. She gained points in the long jump. Jackie lost points in the javelin. She won the last event, the 800 meters. She broke her own heptathlon world record by 76 points.

1. Find a word that has the same consonant blend as in *athlete*. _____
2. What does *heptathlon* mean?
   a. eight events   b. nine events   c. seven events
3. Jackie lost points in the javelin: did she **win** or **lose** that event?
4. Can you lose an event and still win the heptathlon? _____

Day #3

The pentathlon is a five-event course. It was an event in the ancient games. Greece was the site of those ancient games. The ancient games were held about three thousand years ago. Athletes had to run, throw the discus and javelin, jump, and wrestle.

1. You can pronounce the *i* and *e* individually in *ancient*. In which of these words can you also pronounce the *i* and *e* individually: **quiet** or **piece**?
2. What do you think the prefix *pent-* means? a. contest   b. Olympic   c. five
3. Name the five events in the pentathlon. _____
4. The pentathlon was the only event in the ancient games. Is that statement **true** or **false**? _____

Day #4

Flags at the Olympic Games

Can you recognize the Olympic flag? Most people can. The flag has five colored rings. The rings are linked together. They symbolize cooperation and friendship. The flag's background is white. The rings are blue, yellow, black, green, and red. The rings also represent the five parts of the world. Those are Asia, Africa, Europe, Australia, and the Americas.

The flag has been around since 1920. It flies at every Olympics. It flies at the summer and the winter Games. The flag is raised at the opening ceremony. At the end of the Games the flag goes to the next country to host the Olympics.

At the medal ceremonies, flags are raised for the three winners. Those flags are their countries' flags. A band plays the national anthem of the gold medal winner. Athletes carry their countries' flags in the opening ceremonies. It is an honor to carry the flag.

1. Which word has *ie* that is pronounced like **ee**? Which word has an *ie* that is pronounced like a short **e**?

   _____

2. What is the opposite of *honor*?

   _____

3. Which is a better title for this article?

   a. The Olympic Flag

   b. Flags at the Olympics

   Why? _____

4. What are two things the rings represent?

   _____

   _____

   _____

   _____

5. When do we see individual country flags at the Olympics?

   _____

   _____

   _____

   _____

Bonnie Blair

Speed skater Bonnie Blair is the only American woman to have won five Olympic gold medals.

1. What does the title tell us about the subject of this article? _____

2. What is her specialty? _____

3. What is unique about her? _____

4. What country did Bonnie represent at the Olympics? _____

Day #1

Born on March 18, 1964, Bonnie was the youngest in a speed-skating family. Her five older brothers and sisters were champion skaters who encouraged her. They put a pair of skates over Bonnie's shoes when she was two years old because there weren't any skates small enough for her tiny feet.

1. What information do we learn about Bonnie's family? _____

2. What was the effect of Bonnie being born into a speed-skating family?

   _____

3. Does her family sound mean or kind? _____

4. What clues helped you answer #3? _____

Day #2

As Bonnie grew, she trained hard six days a week, always pushing to improve her time. Bonnie kept this up until she was the world's best female speed skater. She won her first Olympic gold medal in the 500-meter race in 1988. In 1992, she won both the 500-meter and the 1,000-meter Olympic races in Albertville, France. She repeated her victories in 1994 in Lillehammer, Norway.

1. What was the effect of Bonnie's practice and hard work? _____

2. How many different Olympics did she compete in? _____

3. What specific events did she compete in? _____

4. How old was Bonnie when she won her last medal? (*Hint:* The Winter Olympics take place in February.) _____

Day #3

Bonnie's Olympic successes made her famous all over the world. Bonnie retired from speed skating in 1995 to focus on other competitions.

1. What was the effect of Bonnie's Olympic successes? _____

2. Why did she retire from speed skating? _____

3. Why would someone retire when she's at the top of her game?

   _____

4. What information that was not in this selection would you like to know about Bonnie Blair? _____

Day #4

1. Do not read the paragraphs. Just looking at the title, do you think it sets up an article about the use of animals at the Olympics or about animals competing at the Olmpics?

_____

Animals at the Olympics

The Olympics are games that show the strength and speed of human athletes. The fastest, strongest person wins. But have you ever wondered what might happen if animals were allowed at the Olympics? Do you still think humans would win?

2. Do not read the next two paragraphs. Do you think humans would win against animals?

_____

The fastest human was clocked at a speed of nearly 27 miles per hour (mph). Many animals can beat that time. A housecat can run 30 mph. The antelope is even faster. It runs at speeds over 60 mph. But the Olympic winner would be the cheetah. This cat runs over 70 mph.

3. Which animals would win the gold, silver, and bronze medals in the running race?

_____

_____

There are two main jumping events in the Olympics. One is height, and the other is distance. The record for the longest human jump is 29 feet. The highest jump without a pole is about 8 feet. The puma would beat humans in both events. It can jump 12 feet high and cover a distance of 39 feet in one jump. However, the animal winning the long jump would the kangaroo. It can jump an amazing 42 feet!

4. What is the difference in feet between a kangaroo's jump and the longest human jump?

_____

_____

5. How does the author feel about the kangaroo's ability to jump?

_____

_____

Sri Lanka is a small island located in the Indian Ocean, near southeast India. The island celebrates a holiday called Poya. Poya has been around since about 250 B.C. Poya honors the full moon. Everything on the island closes for Poya: stores, schools, offices, and movies. The problem is that Poya comes once a month. Why? There's a full moon once a month. Business leaders complain that the holiday disrupts their economy.

1. What word starts with a hard **c** sound? _____

2. What does the word *disrupts* mean?
   a. improves or helps   b. leaves out   c. interrupts or disturbs

3. How many Poya celebrations are there each year?_____

4. Who likes Poya more: **school kids** or **business leaders**? _____

Day #1

The Jewish Sukkoth is an eight-day harvest festival held in September or October. It celebrates the harvest of grapes and olives, two important crops in the Middle East. It is also a time for giving thanks for food and for friendship. Jewish people around the world celebrate Sukkoth. People built wooden booths called Sukkoth. The word also means "shelter."

1. List all the words that start with an **s**/soft **c** sound. _____
2. What does *Sukkoth* mean?_____
3. What is the main idea of this paragraph: **Jewish people build wooden booths** or **Jewish people celebrate a harvest festival they call Sukkoth**?
4. What is the American holiday that is a time for giving thanks for food and for friendship?

Day #2

Many islands have unique styles of music. Some are calypso, ska, reggae, and salsa. Salsa came from Cuba. Calypso is the music of the islands of Trinidad and Tobago. Calypso was influenced by jazz. Ska is from Jamaica. So is reggae. Reggae is a mixture of calypso and rap music.

1. What word ends with the same sound that begins *aeroplane*? _____

2. What does *unique* mean?
   a. strange   b. the only one of its kind   c. popular

3. What is the main subject in this paragraph: **the music** or **the islands**?

4. Which island has two styles of music attributed to it? _____

Day #3

Islands have unique musical instruments. The steel drum originated on Trinidad in the 1930s. Steel drums are called pans. They are made of recycled oil drums. Island music has an African beat. Drums probably came to the islands with African slaves.

Island musicians also use a rhumba box. The rhumba box is like the African thumb piano. It is a wooden box with a hole in the middle. On top are metal keys. Musicians pluck the keys.

1. What word that has to do with poetry starts with *rh* like *rhumba*? _____
2. How do you pluck a musical instrument? _____
3. What is the rhumba box compared with?_____
4. What materials are rhumba boxes made of? _____

Day #4

Pongol

Pongol is a festival in India. It is a rice festival. Rice is an important crop in India. Indians celebrate Pongol in January. This festival falls after the end of the monsoon season, the wet season in India.

The festival lasts three days. People celebrate by cooking and eating newly harvested rice. Families visit neighbors and friends. They share rice treats with them. These sweet treats are made of rice, sugar, and milk. They are called pongol, too.

On the second day of Pongol, Indians decorate their houses for the festival. Women sweep the ground or floor. Then they paint colorful patterns on the cleaned floors or ground. The designs welcome visitors. They use colored rice powder to draw these designs. Sometimes they use colored chalks. The designs are often flower shapes. Some are geometric designs. The lines may be straight or curved. They are called Rangoli or kolam designs.

Rangoli are symmetrical designs. If you draw a line down the middle of the design, one side would look like the other. That line is called the line of symmetry. It's an imaginary line. One side equals the other side.

1. Which words contain a silent *g*?

   _____

   _____

2. What does *symmetrical* mean?

   _____

   _____

3. Do the women draw the line of symmetry on their paintings?

   _____

4. Why do the women paint Rangoli on their floors during Pongol?

   _____

   _____

   _____

5. Is the design on the U.S. flag symmetrical?

   _____

The Crow and the Fox

A crow found a piece of cheese on the ground. It quickly swooped down to pick up the food and perched on a limb to enjoy the tasty treat. A fox wandered by and saw this.

1. This is one of Aesop's fables. What is a fable?
   a. a funny story   b. a true story   c. a story that teaches a lesson

2. What does the title tell us about the characters in this fable? _____

3. Do we meet both characters in the first paragraph? _____

4. What was the first thing the crow did after grabbing the cheese?_____

"Good afternoon, Crow," the fox called out politely. "How lovely you look today! I bet your voice is just as beautiful so that you sing the sweetest melodies of all the birds in the forest."

1. Why was the fox saying nice things to the crow?
   a. he wanted to eat the crow   b. he wanted the cheese
   c. he wanted to hear the crow sing

2. Have you ever heard a crow before? If so, do you think it is a beautiful sound? _____

3. What about the crow did the fox actually compliment?_____

4. What time of day does this fable take place in? _____

The crow believed every word that the fox spoke about her beauty. The crow lifted her beak into the air and opened her mouth to show the fox her musical voice. Just as she did this, the cheese fell out of her mouth. The fox grabbed the cheese and hungrily devoured it.

1. Why did the crow drop the cheese?
   a. she opened her mouth to sing   b. she wanted to share
   c. she wanted to yell at the fox

2. Do you think the fox meant those compliments? _____

3. What was the first thing the fox did after grabbing the cheese? _____

4. What clues tell you that the fox was probably hungrier than the crow?_____

The fox smiled slyly as he walked away, very pleased with his clever trick. As he strolled back into the woods, he called back to the speechless crow, "I will give you some words of wisdom, little Crow. Do not trust those who praise you with so many compliments."

1. Restate the fox's message in your own words._____

2. What other message works?
   a. Always share your cheese.   b. Always compliment others.
   c. Never listen to a fox.

3. Has anyone ever complimented you to get you to do something he or she wanted? If so, did it work? _____

4. Have you ever complimented someone to get what you wanted from him or her? If so, did it work?_____

1. Do you think this one of Aesop's fables? Why or why not?

_____

The Oak and the Reeds

A mighty oak grew along a riverbank. Its trunk was thick, and its branches reached upward into the sky. It towered proudly above a patch of reeds that grew below it along the edge of the water.

2. What kind of thing are the two characters in this fable?

_____

_____

On most days, a breeze blew across the river. The leaves of the mighty oak danced, but its branches held firmly in place. The oak laughed at the reeds because the wind was not so kind to them. The reeds trembled and shook as they struggled to stand up straight. But the reeds did not mind the laughter of the oak; after all, the tree was so much bigger and stronger.

Then one day, a terrible hurricane approached the river. Its violent winds pulled up the roots of the mighty oak and tossed it to the ground. When the storm was over, the great tree lay in the patch of reeds.

3. How is the oak tree different from the reeds?

_____

_____

The oak spoke sadly, "The strong winds were able to pick me up and throw me to the ground like a stick. Yet you reeds were able to stay rooted even though you are much smaller. How could this be?"

One reed spoke. "We may be small, but we know how to bend, whether the wind blows gently or violently. You, mighty oak, were too proud and did not know how to bend."

4. What was the cause of the oak tree falling?

_____

_____

5. What is the lesson of this fable?

   a. It can be better to be flexible than to be strong.

   b. It's okay to laugh at those smaller than you.

   c. Stay out of the way of a hurricane.

Green plants are like factories. Plant factories make two kinds of food: one is sugar, and the other is starch. Almost all fruits and vegetables you eat contain some form of sugar or starch. Fruits like apples, oranges, cherries, pears, and even lemons contain sugar; vegetables like potatoes, corn, and beans contain starch.

1. Circle words with a soft **g** sound and put a line through words with a hard **g** sound.

2. What is a factory? _____

3. With what does the author compare green plants? _____

4. What two kinds of food do plant factories make? _____

Day #1

Green plants are made up of cells just like you are. A cell is the smallest structural unit of a living organism, whether it is a plant or an animal. Because they are so small, cells can be seen only through a microscope. Inside the cells are chloroplasts, which contain chlorophyll and carotene. They manufacture the sugar and starch; therefore, they are the machines of the plant factory.

1. List the words the start with the same starting sound as *clean*. _____

2. With what is a microscope? _____

3. What is compared with the machines of a factory? _____

4. Can you see cells with the naked eye? _____

Day #2

There are two kinds of doors in plant factories. One kind is called stomata. Stomata are tiny holes in the leaves that allow air to move in and out through these doors. Plants use carbon dioxide and then release oxygen back into the air. Roots are the second kind of door. Water travels into root hairs of the plant. This movement is called capillary action.

1. Circle words with *oo* that have the same vowel sound as **boots**. Put a line through words with *oo* containing the same vowel sound as **floor**.

2. What are stomata? _____

3. Which is a better title for this paragraph: **Stomata in the Leaves** or **Doors of the Factory**? _____

4. What are the two kinds of doors in plant factories? _____

Day #3

Plants use storerooms to store their food. Carrot plants store their food in roots, while maple trees store their food in trunks. Lettuce plants store their food in leaves, peas store their food in seeds, and peach trees store their food in the fruit.

1. Find a compound word in this paragraph. _____

2. What word could you use instead of *store* as it is used above? _____

3. What is the topic sentence of this paragraph? _____

4. Name three plants and their storerooms. _____

_____

Day #4

The Brain

Have you ever watched a coach during a ball game? The coach tells players where to go and what to do as things are happening in the game. Your brain is like your coach. Information from your five senses—touch, smell, hearing, taste, sight—races to your brain. Your brain sorts out the information and lets your body know what to do.

Your brain has three main parts, the medulla, cerebrum, and cerebellum. Perhaps you have heard someone talk about "gray matter" while discussing intelligence. This refers to the cerebrum. The cerebrum is large, and its outside layer is gray and looks wrinkled. The cerebrum, the cerebral cortex, springs to work when you are doing something that requires a good deal of thought. If you are taking a test, talking to a friend, or reading directions to put together a new bicycle, your cerebrum is busy.

As you try to keep your balance on your bicycle, it is your cerebellum that is called to work. The cerebellum is in control of balance and coordination. It is much smaller than the cerebrum.

The medulla is your brain stem. It is the lowest part of your brain. The medulla controls breathing and heart rate.

The next time you put together a bicycle, and then hop on and gasp for breath after riding up a hill, you will know that all the parts of your brain have been very busy.

1. List the words that have to do with the brain that start with a soft **c** sound.

   _____

2. What is the cerebral cortex?

   _____

   _____

3. To what does the idiom *gray matter* refer?

   _____

   _____

4. What does this article compare your brain with? Why?

   _____

   _____

5. Make a chart that details which part of the brain controls which function and one example of that function.

Aboriginal Art

The Aboriginal people in Australia were hunters and gatherers. They were also skilled artists. They have been painting and carving rocks for thousands of years. The paintings are found mostly in caves throughout central Australia. The oldest paintings that have been discovered are about 30,000 years old.

1. What does the title tell us about the subject of this article? _____
2. Where do Aborigines live? _____
3. What details does the paragraph tell you about them? _____
4. Aborigines are the original dwellers of Australia. What do they compare with in the United States? _____

Day #1

Aborigine artists use natural paints made from the earth, tree bark, and plants. Red comes from ochre and hematite. Ochre and hematite are minerals. Black comes from charcoal. White comes from gypsum, a mineral found in rocks. It's used to make cement.

1. Where does the paragraph tell us Aborigine artists find their paints? _____
2. What is the one example of a color that does not come from a mineral? _____
3. Does this paragraph give you any examples of colors from plants? _____
4. What do Aborigine paintings have in common with cement? _____
_____

Day #2

Aborigine musicians have unusual musical instruments. One is called the didgeridoo. It is made from a hollowed-out log. It is a wind instrument that is played by blowing wind through it. A didgeridoo may be painted with the same elaborate designs found in the rock paintings.

1. So far, in this article, what two things do Aborigine artists paint? _____
2. Does the didgeridoo sound like it is a small or a large instrument? _____
3. Did Aborigine musicians find their musical instruments like the artists found their paints—from nature? _____
4. What clues helped you answer #3? _____

Day #3

Aborigines paint themselves for special religious ceremonies. These ceremonies are a part of their traditional culture. Their religion links them to the land and nature. They express themselves artistically through music making, dancing, singing, and storytelling.

1. List all the things the article says Aborigine artists paint on. _____
2. What is important to their religion? _____
3. What do Aborigine people do in their religious ceremonies? _____
_____
4. How does painting come into their religious ceremonies?

Day #4

Assessment

1. What would you guess the topic of this article is, just based on the title?

_____

Dreamtime

The Aborigines have been in Australia for thousands of years. Some scientists believe they have been there for about 30,000 years. The name *Aborigine* means "the very first." They were the very first people in Australia. They believe that ancestral beings created the world in a time very long ago, called Dreamtime. Elders know the history of Dreamtime. They pass it on to younger generations.

2. What is the Dreamtime in this article? Was it what you expected from the title?

_____

_____

Dreamtime explains the beginning of the world. Aborigines believe that during Dreamtime, spirits created the land, animals, plants, and humans. The spirit beings didn't die. They joined with nature. They live in the Aborigine beliefs and sacred rituals. Dreamtime explains the rules for living. It explains the rules for social behavior. It explains the whole structure of society.

3. List all the things the second paragraph says Aborigines believe Dreamtime explains.

_____

_____

_____

Dreamtime paintings are usually symmetrical. They are made of arcs, circles, and ovals. Some lines are straight. Some are curved. Specific patterns and designs have names. The men paint Dreamtime symbols and patterns on their bodies for special ceremonies. The ceremonies are called corroborees.

4. Name the geometric shapes used in Dreamtime paintings.

_____

5. What clues from the article tell you that Dreamtime has a central place in Aborigine life and culture?

_____

_____

_____

Teddy just about fell out of his seat that Monday afternoon.

Mrs. Beeker, his science teacher, announced to the class that during the following week, they would go to the Colgate Nature Preserve to examine the pond life in Dilly Pond! That meant he'd be free to splash away in the water in search of his beloved leopard frogs!

1. Which letter in *leopard* is silent? _____
2. When is *the following week*?
   a. that week   b. the next week   c. two weeks from then
3. What effect did the news of his class trip have on Teddy? _____
4. What do you think a leopard frog looks like? _____

The next week the class boarded the waiting bus in front of the school and rode off to Dilly Pond. Students scooped and troweled for larvae, crustaceans, and small fish. They sketched pictures of plants in and near the pond. They observed birds, mammals, and amphibians. And Teddy? He mucked around in the rushes among the creatures of frog heaven.

1. Which word ends with the same ending as *oceans*? _____
2. What does *troweled* mean? _____
3. List all the items the kids interacted with in the wetlands. _____
4. What does the author mean by **frog heaven: heaven for dead frogs** or **heaven for Teddy the frog-lover**? _____

That was thirty years ago. But Teddy still remembers. As he prepares the science laboratory for his students, his mind returns to the pond that glorious fall day so many years ago. It was the day that he first knew what he wanted to do with his life. It was one of the best days he could remember.

1. Does the *ou* in *glorious* sound like the *ou* in **out** or **serious**? _____
2. What other word (two syllables or more) could you use instead of *glorious*?

   _____

3. What is Teddy's job today? _____
4. What effect did the field trip have on Teddy's life? _____

With a whimper, Daisy hung her head and looked at me beseechingly.

1. *Beseechingly* has two suffixes. What are they? _____
2. When Daisy looks beseechingly, is she **begging** or **angry**? _____
3. Does Daisy sound happy? What clues helped you answer that question?

   _____

4. What do you think Daisy is? _____

0-7682-3214-7 *Read 4 Today*

Aquarium Competition

Jake opened the lid of his aquarium. Most of the fish quickly swam to the top. They knew it was time for dinner. Jake paused before sprinkling the food across the water. He noticed that one little fish stayed away from the others. Its fins were looking ragged. Jake wondered whether the fish might be sick.

Jake tapped the can, and the food fell out. He saw one big fish rush to the top and gobble most of the food. This same fish nipped at the fins of the smaller fish whenever it tried to grab a bite.

"I see why the fins are ragged," thought Jake. "That little fish isn't sick at all. The bigger fish is just picking on it."

Jake got out a smaller fish bowl. He poured some tank water into the bowl, scooped the ragged fish out of the aquarium with a net, and gently put it in the small bowl.

"There you go, little guy!" said Jake. "I'll give you lots of food and some time to grow. When you get big and strong, I'll put you back in the aquarium again. Then you will be able to compete with that bully fish!"

1. Find a word that begins with a soft **g** sound.

   _____

2. What does it mean to be a bully?

   _____

   _____

3. What is the effect of the big fish gobbling up all the food?

   _____

   _____

4. In this story, what does *compete* mean?

   a. to get to the top of the tank faster

   b. to be a bigger bully

   c. to grow bigger than the others

5. Try to predict what will happen to the little, ragged fish now.

   _____

   _____

Animal Mysteries

As long as people have studied animals, they have wondered why animals act certain ways. Animal behavior can be a real mystery.

1. What does the title tell us about the topic of this article? _____
2. What kind of mystery is the topic here? _____
3. How do people come across these mysterious behaviors? _____
4. What is a mystery? _____

One mystery has to do with some animals' strange behavior before earthquakes. Horses and cattle stampede, seabirds screech, dogs howl, and some animals even come out of hibernation early before an earthquake begins.

1. What is the first mystery? _____
2. What specific details does the author include? _____
3. Why might it be helpful to know about these behaviors if you lived in earthquake country? _____
4. Is the behavior for each animal something it doesn't do normally? Or is it unusual that the animal behave this way right before an earthquake? _____

Another mystery involves birds and ants. No one can explain why a bird will pick up an ant in its beak and rub the ant over its feathers again and again. This is called "anting," and birds have been known to do this for an hour without stopping.

1. What is the mystery in this paragraph? _____
2. Does the activity have a special name? If so, what is it? _____
3. Do any words give you the idea that the author finds this mystery funny?

   _____
4. Do you find it funny? Why or why not? _____

One animal mystery is very sad. For hundreds of years, some whales have swum into shallow waters and mysteriously grounded themselves on a beach where they might die. Reports of beached whales occur about five times a year somewhere in the world.

1. What is the mystery in this paragraph? _____
2. Does the author give an opinion about this mystery? _____
3. If so, what opinion? _____
4. How do you think the author feels about animals? _____

 0-7682-3214-7 *Read 4 Today*

1. Without reading the poem, what do you already know about backpacks?

_____

My Backpack
Anonymous

2. Does the title tell you the name of the person who wrote this poem?

_____

My backpack's so heavy
It must weigh a ton.
With thousands of books—
My work's never done

My arms are so sore
I can't lift a pen.
My breath is so short
I need oxygen.

When I stoop over,
It makes me fall down.
I think I'll just stay here
All squashed on the ground.

3. Why would the writer describe his or her feelings in this way?

_____

_____

4. What was the effect of the heavy backpack?

_____

_____

5. What decision has the author made?

_____

_____

Have you ever had the pleasure of watching a praying mantis capture its prey? It raises its forelegs, as if in prayer, and waits patiently for an unsuspecting insect. When its prey comes within striking distance, the mantis thrusts its forelegs out and grabs its insect victim. The clever praying mantis is actually a preying master.

1. Which two words sound the same but are spelled differently?

   _____

2. What does the prefix *un-* in *unsuspecting* mean?_____

3. What words does the author use to refer to the insect?_____

4. Why is it called a *praying* mantis? _____

Day #1

A mantis relies on its keen vision for capturing prey. Its triangular face supports two huge compound eyes. The mantis may tilt its head as if to get a better look at you, but its compound eyes allow it to see in almost all directions. In the center of its two eyes, the mantis also has three other tiny eyes, called ocelli, which help the mantis distinguish dark and light.

1. Does the *gu* in *distinguish* sound like the *gu* in **guide** or **anguish**?_____

2. What word could you use instead of *keen*? _____

3. What is the main subject of this paragraph? _____

4. What does it mean that the mantis has *compound eyes*? _____

Day #2

In the early morning or late afternoon, you may find a praying mantis hanging upside down with its forelegs folded. It is not resting; the mantis is waiting. It is waiting for a fly, bee, butterfly, grasshopper, or caterpillar. The mantis eats only insects. It has no need even for water since it gets plenty from the body of its prey.

1. Name at least three kinds of prey for a mantis._____

2. Does the prefix *fore-* in *forelegs* mean **four** or **front**? _____

3. Are you likely to find a praying mantis hanging upside down at noon? _____

4. How does the praying mantis get water? _____

Day #3

When it captures its prey, the mantis bites off and discards the head, eating the insect alive. Mantises are cannibals. After mating, the female mantis will often eat her mate simply because he is the nearest insect.

1. The plural of *mantis* is _____.

2. Is a cannibal something that eats its prey alive or something that eats its own kind?_____

3. What is a good title for this paragraph?_____

4. What is your advice to a male mantis after mating: stay awhile or get out of there? _____

Day #4

Echo-Echo!

Perhaps you have heard that many types of bats have very small eyes and do not see well. Still, as they swoop through the night, they do not bump into objects and are able to find food, even though they cannot see their prey. How is this possible? Echolocation. You might recognize the beginning of the word *echolocation* as "echo," and you might recognize the last part of the word as "location." This gives you clues about how echolocation works. The bat sends out sounds. The sounds bounce off objects and return to the bat. Echolocation not only tells the bat that objects are nearby. It also tells the bat just how far away the objects are. Bats are not the only creatures that use echolocation. Porpoises and some types of whales and birds use it as well.

1. Use the **ch** sound in *echolocation* to begin another word.

   _____

2. What is echolocation?

   _____

   _____

   _____

3. Which word in this passage sounds like what it means?

   a. objects
   b. bat
   c. swoop

4. How does echolocation work?

   _____

   _____

   _____

5. List the animals that use echolocation.

   _____

   _____

   _____

Those Wacky Australian Animals

Australia's animals are unique. Australia has marsupials and monotremes. Marsupials are animals that carry their babies in pouches. A marsupial baby crawls into its mother's pouch and stays there until it is much bigger. Monotremes are mammals that give birth to their young by laying eggs, but they produce milk to feed their babies.

1. What clues does the title give us about the subject of this article? _____

2. What word in the title tells us the author has a sense of humor about the article? _____

3. What is distinctive about monotremes? _____

4. What is distinctive about marsupials? _____

Day #1

The Tasmanian devil is a ferocious marsupial that lives on the island of Tasmania. These animals have black fur and very sharp teeth. They eat other mammals, birds, and reptiles.

1. What kind of animal is the Tasmanian devil? _____

2. What clues does the paragraph give you that is deserves the name *devil*?

_____

3. How did the *Tasmanian* part of the animal's name come about? _____

4. Is the Tasmanian devil a carnivore? _____

Day #2

The duck-billed platypus is one of two animals that hatches its young from eggs. It has soft fur, a snout, webbed feet and claws, and a flat tail like a beaver's tail. They live near rivers and creeks, where they eat crawfish, worms, and small fish.

1. What kind of animal is the duck-billed platypus? _____

2. What animal is compared with the duck-billed platypus in the paragraph?

_____

3. List the characteristics of the duck-billed platypus. List other animals that share one characteristic. You may want to make a chart. _____

4. What do you think of the duck-billed platypus's looks? _____

Day #3

Kangaroos are herbivores. Baby kangaroos, called joeys, live in their mother's pouch for 5 to 6 months. Kangaroos can hop at about 40 miles per hour (about 64.3 kph). They have strong hind legs for leaping about 30 to 40 feet (about 9 to 12 m).

1. What does a herbivore eat?
   a. meat   b. plants   c. metal

2. What kind of animal is a kangaroo? _____

3. How does a kangaroo get around? _____

4. Is the author right: Are Australian animals wacky? _____

Day #4

Assessment

1. This title gives a lot of information. What does it tell us the author will do in this article?

   _____

Australia and the United States: Alike or Different?

How are Australia and the United States alike? How are they different? Australia is in the Southern Hemisphere. The United States is in the Northern Hemisphere. That means Australia's summer months are December through February, which are our winter months. Our summer months are June through August, which are their winter months. In the Northern Hemisphere, hurricanes and tornadoes spin in a clockwise direction. In the Southern Hemisphere they spin in a counterclockwise direction.

2. If you had a birthday on December 11, compare the activities you could do at your birthday party if you lived in Australia and if you lived in the United States.

   _____

   _____

Australians drive on the left side of the road, while we drive on the right side of the road. Australia's population is about 19 million. That's about the same as the six most populated cities in the United States. Australia has kangaroos, anteaters, emus, and koalas, but here you'll find those animals only in zoos.

3. Do more people live in Australia or in the United States?

   _____

The official head of Australia's government is the queen of England. Ours is the President. Australians elect people to a legislature, and a prime minister is the functional head of government. There are three major political parties there, but only two here. An Australian law says that people who are able to vote must vote. If not, they can be fined. There's no law like that in the United States.

4. Put the following topics in the order they appear in the article: population, politics, climate, wildlife, customs.

   _____

   _____

5. What do you think is the most interesting difference between Australia and the United States?

   _____

   _____

Answer Key

Tanner and Nick were roller-skating down the sidewalk. Nick hit a stone and fell. His knees and hands slammed into the ground. It was a good thing he was wearing kneepads. His hands were another story.

Day #1

1. Find a word in the paragraph that starts with a silent consonant. __kneepads__
2. What is another word you could use instead of *slammed*? __fell, bumped, scraped__
3. What was the effect of Nick hitting a stone while roller-skating? _____
   He fell.
4. What happened to Nick's hands? __His hands were badly scraped__

Only three problems out of his thirty-two were done. For the past half-hour Dan had been looking at the page and daydreaming. "Hey, pass your paper up," said Joe. "Mrs. Willis just asked for our work."

Day #2

1. Find a word that is made up of two other words. __daydreaming__
2. What is another way to say *half hour*? __thirty minutes__
3. *Pass* is a homograph, a word that can be used different ways. Circle the use here that is used the same way as in our paragraph: "I passed the test anyway!" or (Pass me the butter.")
4. Who is Mrs. Willis? __She is Dan's teacher.__

Bonnie Butterfly flew through the air. She could see for miles. Bonnie was exhausted and (hungry) and she wanted to land. (She felt very comfortable flying, but landing) (was still hard for her.) She caught sight of a patch of delicious-looking flowers. "Oh dear," she thought. "Do I dare land there?"

Day #3

1. Circle the word in the paragraph that has the same consonant blend as *angry*.
2. What does *exhausted* mean? __really tired__
3. What does *dare* mean to Bonnie? Did another butterfly dare her to land there?
   No. It means she's nervous about landing
4. Bonnie Butterfly has only just learned how to fly. Circle the sentence that tells you that. She felt very comfortable flying.

Have you ever listened to the sweet strings of symphony violins? Perhaps you have heard the (light) melody of the flutes. Or maybe you have heard the (ping) of harp strings. The musicians in the orchestra are seated in special places to make the music sound just (right.)

Day #4

1. Circle the words that rhyme with *fight*.
2. What is a symphony? __a large group of musicians who play violins, flutes, harps, and other instruments__
3. Some words sound like what they mean. As your teacher reads the paragraph out loud, circle the word or words that sound like what they mean.
4. Is a symphony the same as an orchestra? __yes__

Assessment

Salt and Pepper

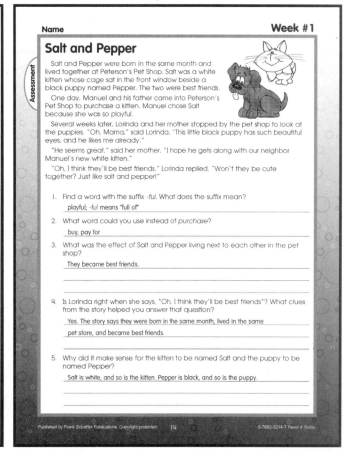

Salt and Pepper were born in the same month and lived together at Peterson's Pet Shop. Salt was a white kitten whose cage sat in the front window beside a black puppy named Pepper. The two were best friends.

One day, Manuel and his father came into Peterson's Pet Shop to purchase a kitten. Manuel chose Salt because she was so playful.

Several weeks later, Lorinda and her mother stopped by the pet shop to look at the puppies. "Oh, Mama," said Lorinda. "This little black puppy has such beautiful eyes, and he likes me already."

"He seems great," said her mother. "I hope he gets along with our neighbor Manuel's new white kitten."

"Oh, I think they'll be best friends," Lorinda replied. "Won't they be cute together? Just like salt and pepper!"

1. Find a word with the suffix *-ful*. What does the suffix mean?
   playful; *-ful* means "full of"
2. What word could you use instead of *purchase*?
   buy, pay for
3. What was the effect of Salt and Pepper living next to each other in the pet shop?
   They became best friends.
4. Is Lorinda right when she says, "Oh, I think they'll be best friends"? What clues from the story helped you answer that question?
   Yes. The story says they were born in the same month, lived in the same
   pet store, and became best friends.
5. Why did it make sense for the kitten to be named Salt and the puppy to be named Pepper?
   Salt is white, and so is the kitten. Pepper is black, and so is the puppy.

Tree Needs

Dave was helping his dad plant some ash trees in the yard.

Day #1

1. What does the title tell us about what the subject of the passage might be?
   trees
2. Does the title say anything specific about the subject? __trees have needs__
3. What does the opening sentence tell us about who is in this passage?
   Dave and his dad
4. What are they doing? __They are planting trees.__

Dave picked up the shovel and walked over to the place where they had laid out the last tree. He pushed the shovel into the ground. The point wouldn't go in, so Dave tried jumping on the shovel.
"Dad, the ground here is so hard I can't get the blade in the soil," said Dave.

Day #2

1. Is there a problem in this passage? If so, what is it? __Yes. Dave can't get the shovel__ blade into the hard ground.
2. Does a character try to solve the problem? __yes__
3. If so, what does the character do? __He jumps on the shovel and then tells his dad.__
4. Did you find out more about the subject we guessed from the title? __no__

Mr. Ruiz came and looked at the ground. "We may need to find another place to plant this tree," he said. "Like all plants, trees need four things—sunlight, air, water, and good soil. While there is plenty of sunlight, this place may lack the soil, water, and air that the tree needs."

Day #3

1. Has a new character entered the story? If so, what is that character's name?
   No, but I can infer that Mr. Ruiz is Dave's dad.
2. What is the effect of the problem? __They have to find a new place to plant the tree.__
3. Did you find out more about the subject we guessed from the title? __yes__
4. If so, what have you discovered? __Trees need sunlight, soil, water, and air.__

Mr. Ruiz slowly walked around the yard. Every once in a while, he poked the point of the shovel into the dirt to test the soil. Soon the shovel blade sliced easily into the dirt. "I think we just found a new home for this last tree," said Mr. Ruiz. "Do you see this soil? It's loose and black, which means there are lots of nutrients in it. And with the soil being loose, the water and air can easily drain down to the tree's roots."

Day #4

1. Did the characters solve the problem? __Yes, they found a new place for the tree.__
2. If so, how did they solve it? __They kept trying until they found a place that worked.__
3. Were there any more details about the subject in the last paragraph? If so, what? __Yes; trees like loose soil with lots of nutrients.__
4. Was this a story or a science article? __a story__

Assessment

1. Do the title and opening paragraph remind you of a fairy tale you know? If so, which fairy tale?
   yes; "Goldilocks and the Three Bears"

The Goldilocks Report

At 5:05 p.m., we were called to the home of a Mr. and Mrs. Bear.

2. Who is involved in this story? __Goldilocks, Mr. and Mrs. Bear, Officer Paws,__
   another officer

They had been out for the day. Upon returning home, they found the lock on their door had been broken. Officer Paws and I went into the house. We found that food had been stolen and a chair had been broken.

3. What is the problem in the story? __Mr. and Mrs. Bear found their lock broken,__
   and the officers found that food was gone and a chair broken.

Paws searched the back yard while I went upstairs. I found a person asleep in a small bed. The subject was a female human with curly, blonde hair. She was unknown to the Bear family. The human claimed her name was Goldilocks. She could not prove that fact. She will be questioned at the police station.

4. How is the solution to the problem in this story different from the end of the story in the fairy tale?
   In this story, the police take Goldilocks to the police station for questioning.
   In the fairytale, Goldilocks runs away.
5. Who is in this story but is not in the fairy tale? __the two police officers__

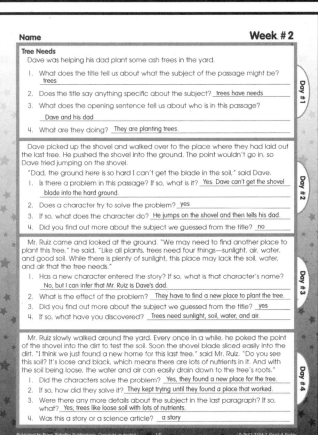

Answer Key

Week #3 — Day pages

There are more than 15,000 active volcanoes in the world. Still, scientists don't know everything there is to know about volcanoes. The study of volcanoes is called volcanology, and people who study volcanoes are called volcanologists.

Day #1

1. Find a word in the paragraph that has a silent consonant. __scientists__
2. What is volcanology? __Volcanology is the study of volcanoes.__
3. Read the paragraph silently as the teacher reads it aloud to the class. Name one big idea from the paragraph. __There are 15,000 active volcanoes. This paragraph is about the study of volcanoes.__
4. What does a volcanologist do? __A volcanologist studies volcanoes.__

Earth and Venus are planets that have volcanoes. Venus has more volcanoes than any other planet. Scientists have mapped more than 1,600 volcanoes on Venus. Some scientists believe that there may be more than one million volcanoes on the planet.

Day #2

1. Does the beginning sound of the word *earth* sound more like *ear* or more like the vowel sound in *birth*? __birth__
2. What is the opposite of *more*? __less, fewer__
3. Compare Venus with Earth. Which planet does the paragraph tell us has more volcanoes? __Venus__
4. Have scientists found all the volcanoes they think are on Venus? __no__

The Richter Scale was developed by Charles Richter. It compares the size of earthquakes. The scale tells us how big or serious an earthquake is. This is the earthquake's magnitude. A magnitude of 4.0–4.9 means that people can feel the earthquake but it does little damage. A magnitude of 6.0–6.9 means the earthquake can cause a great deal of damage in a large area.

Day #3

1. Circle each word that has three or more syllables. __developed, magnitude (3 times)__
2. What does *magnitude* mean? __the size or seriousness of an earthquake__
3. What is the effect of a magnitude 4.5 earthquake? __People can feel the earthquake, but it does little damage.__
4. What does it mean as the numbers get higher? __The earthquake is more serious; it does more damage.__

Until scientists can determine when earthquakes will happen, people can take action to protect themselves. In 1994, an earthquake struck in Northridge, California. A fault deep below the surface caused the earthquake. Scientists did not even know that the fault existed.

Day #4

1. What word has a silent consonant? __scientists__
2. What word could you use instead of *message*: **letter** or **information**? __information__
3. Does the paragraph tell us that scientists know everything? __no__
4. What clue from the paragraph helped you answer #3? __Scientists didn't know about the fault in Northridge until the earthquake happened.__

Week #3 — Assessment

Pompeii

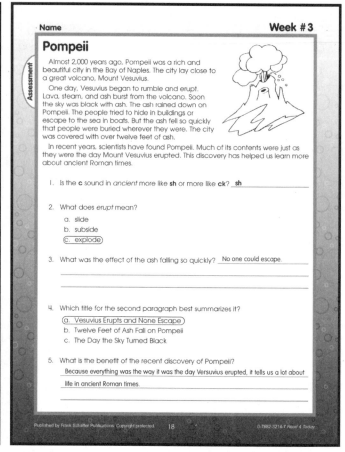

Almost 2,000 years ago, Pompeii was a rich and beautiful city in the Bay of Naples. The city lay close to a great volcano, Mount Vesuvius.

One day, Vesuvius began to rumble and erupt. Lava, steam, and ash burst from the volcano. Soon the sky was black with ash. The ash rained down on Pompeii. The people tried to hide in buildings or escape to the sea in boats. But the ash fell so quickly that people were buried wherever they were. The city was covered with over twelve feet of ash.

In recent years, scientists have found Pompeii. Much of its contents were just as they were the day Mount Vesuvius erupted. This discovery has helped us learn more about ancient Roman times.

1. Is the **c** sound in *ancient* more like **sh** or more like **ck**? __sh__

2. What does *erupt* mean?
   a. slide
   b. subside
   c. explode ⟵ (circled)

3. What was the effect of the ash falling so quickly? __No one could escape.__

4. Which title for the second paragraph best summarizes it?
   a. Vesuvius Erupts and None Escape ⟵ (circled)
   b. Twelve Feet of Ash Fall on Pompeii
   c. The Day the Sky Turned Black

5. What is the benefit of the recent discovery of Pompeii? __Because everything was the way it was the day Versuvius erupted, it tells us a lot about life in ancient Roman times.__

Week #4 — Day pages

The Underground Railroad

The Underground Railroad wasn't a railroad at all. It was a group of people who helped slaves escape to freedom. Those in charge of the escape effort were often called "conductors." The people escaping were known as "passengers." And the places where the escaping slaves stopped for help were often called "stations."

Day #1

1. Cover the opening sentence with your hand. What do you think the title alone tells you about what the subject of the selection might be? __a train that travels underground__
2. Does the opening sentence support or contradict your guess? __contradict__
3. What is the subject of this selection? __the people who helped slaves escape__
4. What does the opening paragraph tell us about who is involved? __the slaves and the people who helped them__

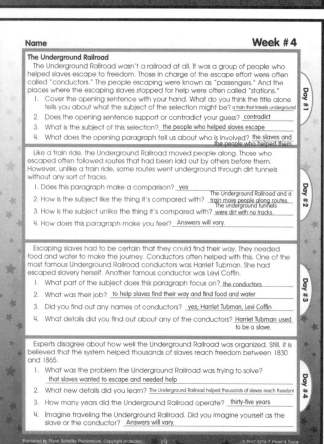

Like a train ride, the Underground Railroad moved people along. Those who escaped often followed routes that had been laid out by others before them. However, unlike a train ride, some routes went underground through dirt tunnels without any sort of tracks.

Day #2

1. Does this paragraph make a comparison? __yes__
2. How is the subject like the thing it's compared with? __The Underground Railroad and a train move people along routes.__
3. How is the subject unlike the thing it's compared with? __The underground tunnels were dirt with no tracks.__
4. How does this paragraph make you feel? __Answers will vary.__

Escaping slaves had to be certain that they could find their way. They needed food and water to make the journey. Conductors often helped with this. One of the most famous Underground Railroad conductors was Harriet Tubman. She had escaped slavery herself. Another famous conductor was Levi Coffin.

Day #3

1. What part of the subject does this paragraph focus on? __the conductors__
2. What was their job? __to help slaves find their way and find food and water__
3. Did you find out any names of conductors? __yes; Harriet Tubman, Levi Coffin__
4. What details did you find out about any of the conductors? __Harriet Tubman used to be a slave.__

Experts disagree about how well the Underground Railroad was organized. Still, it is believed that the system helped thousands of slaves reach freedom between 1830 and 1865.

Day #4

1. What was the problem the Underground Railroad was trying to solve? __that slaves wanted to escape and needed help__
2. What new details did you learn? __The Underground Railroad helped thousands of slaves reach freedom.__
3. How many years did the Underground Railroad operate? __thirty-five years__
4. Imagine traveling the Underground Railroad. Did you imagine yourself as the slave or the conductor? __Answers will vary.__

Week #4 — Assessment

Quilts Reflect a Culture

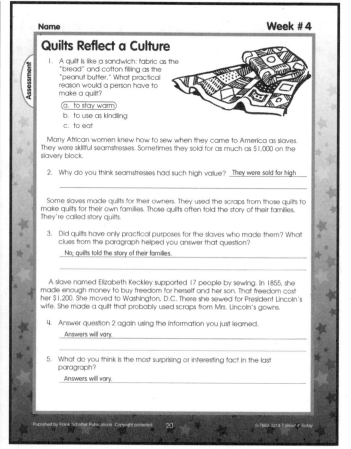

1. A quilt is like a sandwich: fabric as the "bread" and cotton filling as the "peanut butter." What practical reason would a person have to make a quilt?
   a. to stay warm ⟵ (circled)
   b. to use as kindling
   c. to eat

Many African women knew how to sew when they came to America as slaves. They were skillful seamstresses. Sometimes they sold for as much as $1,000 on the slavery block.

2. Why do you think seamstresses had such high value? __They were sold for high__

Some slaves made quilts for their owners. They used the scraps from those quilts to make quilts for their own families. Those quilts often told the story of their families. They're called story quilts.

3. Did quilts have only practical purposes for the slaves who made them? What clues from the paragraph helped you answer that question? __No; quilts told the story of their families.__

A slave named Elizabeth Keckley supported 17 people by sewing. In 1855, she made enough money to buy freedom for herself and her son. That freedom cost her $1,200. She moved to Washington, D.C. There she sewed for President Lincoln's wife. She made a quilt that probably used scraps from Mrs. Lincoln's gowns.

4. Answer question 2 again using the information you just learned. __Answers will vary.__

5. What do you think is the most surprising or interesting fact in the last paragraph? __Answers will vary.__

Answer Key

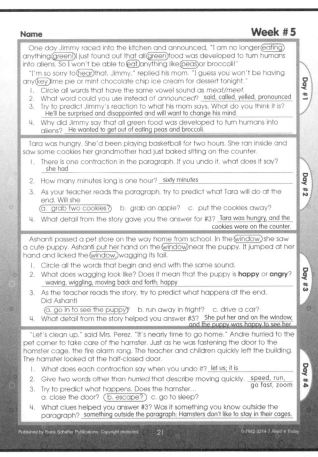

Day #1

One day Jimmy raced into the kitchen and announced, "I am no longer (eating) anything (green). I just found out that all (green) food was developed to turn humans into aliens. So I won't be able to (eat) anything like (peas) or broccoli!"

"I'm so sorry to (hear) that, Jimmy," replied his mom. "I guess you won't be having any (key) lime pie or mint chocolate chip ice cream for dessert tonight."

1. Circle all words that have the same vowel sound as *meat/meet*.
2. What word could you use instead of *announced*? _said, called, yelled, pronounced_
3. Try to predict Jimmy's reaction to what his mom says. What do you think it is? _He'll be surprised and disappointed and will want to change his mind._
4. Why did Jimmy say that all green food was developed to turn humans into aliens? _He wanted to get out of eating peas and broccoli._

Day #2

Tara was hungry. She'd been playing basketball for two hours. She ran inside and saw some cookies her grandmother had just baked sitting on the counter.

1. There is one contraction in the paragraph. If you undo it, what does it say? _she had_
2. How many minutes long is one hour? _sixty minutes_
3. As your teacher reads the paragraph, try to predict what Tara will do at the end. Will she
   (a. grab two cookies?) b. grab an apple? c. put the cookies away?
4. What detail from the story gave you the answer for #3? _Tara was hungry, and the cookies were on the counter._

Day #3

Ashanti passed a pet store on the way home from school. In the (window) she saw a cute puppy. Ashanti put her hand on the (window) near the puppy. It jumped at her hand and licked the (window) wagging its tail.

1. Circle all the words that begin and end with the same sound.
2. What does wagging look like? Does it mean that the puppy is **happy** or **angry**? _waving, wiggling, moving back and forth; happy_
3. As the teacher reads the story, try to predict what happens at the end. Did Ashanti
   (a. go in to see the puppy?) b. run away in fright? c. drive a car?
4. What detail from the story helped you answer #3? _She put her and on the window, and the puppy was happy to see her._

Day #4

"Let's clean up," said Mrs. Perez. "It's nearly time to go home." Andre hurried to the pet corner to take care of the hamster. Just as he was fastening the door to the hamster cage, the fire alarm rang. The teacher and children quickly left the building. The hamster looked at the half-closed door.

1. What does each contraction say when you undo it? _let us; it is_
2. Give two words other than *hurried* that describe moving quickly. _speed, run, go fast, zoom_
3. Try to predict what happens. Does the hamster…
   a. close the door? (b. escape?) c. go to sleep?
4. What clues helped you answer #3? Was it something you know outside the paragraph? _something outside the paragraph: Hamsters don't like to stay in their cages._

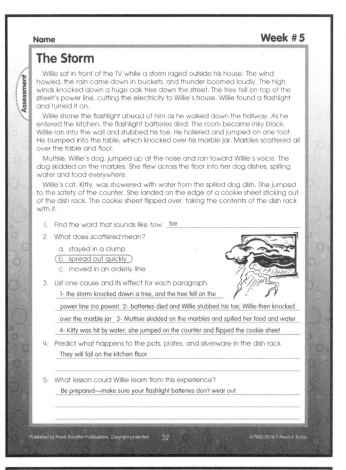

Assessment

The Storm

Willie sat in front of the TV while a storm raged outside his house. The wind howled, the rain came down in buckets, and thunder boomed loudly. The high winds knocked down a huge oak tree down the street. The tree fell on top of the street's power line, cutting the electricity to Willie's house. Willie found a flashlight and turned it on.

Willie shone the flashlight ahead of him as he walked down the hallway. As he entered the kitchen, the flashlight batteries died. The room became inky black. Willie ran into the wall and stubbed his toe. He hollered and jumped on one foot. He bumped into the table, which knocked over his marble jar. Marbles scattered all over the table and floor.

Muttsie, Willie's dog, jumped up at the noise and ran toward Willie's voice. The dog skidded on the marbles. She flew across the floor into her dog dishes, spilling water and food everywhere.

Willie's cat, Kitty, was showered with water from the spilled dog dish. She jumped to the safety of the counter. She landed on the edge of a cookie sheet sticking out of the dish rack. The cookie sheet flipped over, taking the contents of the dish rack with it.

1. Find the word that sounds like *tow*. _toe_
2. What does *scattered* mean?
   a. stayed in a clump
   (b. spread out quickly)
   c. moved in an orderly line
3. List one cause and its effect for each paragraph.
   1- the storm knocked down a tree, and the tree fell on the power line (no power) 2- batteries died and Willie stubbed his toe; Willie then knocked over the marble jar 3- Muttsie skidded on the marbles and spilled her food and water 4- Kitty was hit by water; she jumped on the counter and flipped the cookie sheet
4. Predict what happens to the pots, plates, and silverware in the dish rack. _They will fall on the kitchen floor._
5. What lesson could Willie learn from this experience? _Be prepared—make sure your flashlight batteries don't wear out._

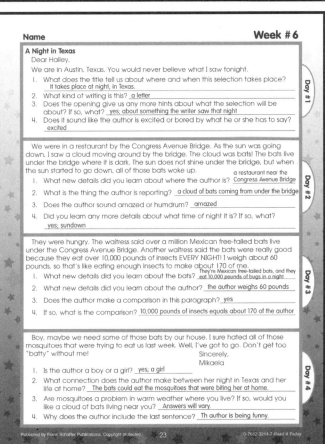

Day #1

A Night in Texas

Dear Hailey,

We are in Austin, Texas. You would never believe what I saw tonight.

1. What does the title tell us about where and when this selection takes place? _It takes place at night, in Texas._
2. What kind of writing is this? _a letter_
3. Does the opening give us any more hints about what the selection will be about? If so, what? _yes; about something the writer saw that night_
4. Does it sound like the author is excited or bored by what he or she has to say? _excited_

Day #2

We were in a restaurant by the Congress Avenue Bridge. As the sun was going down, I saw a cloud moving around by the bridge. The cloud was bats! The bats live under the bridge where it is dark. The sun does not shine under the bridge, but when the sun started to go down, all of those bats woke up.

1. What new details did you learn about where the author is? _a restaurant near the Congress Avenue Bridge_
2. What is the thing the author is reporting? _a cloud of bats coming from under the bridge_
3. Does the author sound amazed or humdrum? _amazed_
4. Did you learn any more details about what time of night it is? If so, what? _yes; sundown_

Day #3

They were hungry. The waitress said over a million Mexican free-tailed bats live under the Congress Avenue Bridge. Another waitress said the bats were really good because they eat over 10,000 pounds of insects EVERY NIGHT! I weigh about 60 pounds, so that's like eating about 170 of me.

1. What new details did you learn about the bats? _They're Mexican free-tailed bats, and they eat 10,000 pounds of bugs in a night_
2. What new details did you learn about the author? _the author weighs 60 pounds_
3. Does the author make a comparison in this paragraph? _yes_
4. If so, what is the comparison? _10,000 pounds of insects equals about 170 of the author_

Day #4

Boy, maybe we need some of those bats by our house. I sure hated all of those mosquitoes that were trying to eat us last week. Well, I've got to go. Don't get too "batty" without me!

Sincerely,
Mikaela

1. Is the author a boy or a girl? _yes; a girl_
2. What connection does the author make between her night in Texas and her life at home? _The bats could eat the mosquitoes that were biting her at home._
3. Are mosquitoes a problem in warm weather where you live? If so, would you like a cloud of bats living near you? _Answers will vary._
4. Why does the author include the last sentence? _Th author is being funny._

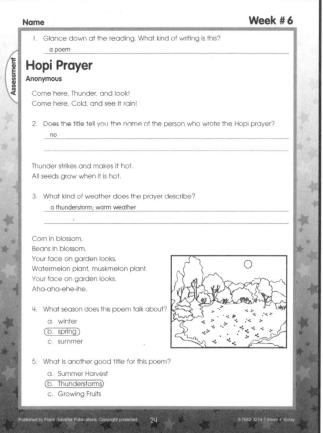

Assessment

1. Glance down at the reading. What kind of writing is this? _a poem_

Hopi Prayer
Anonymous

Come here, Thunder, and look!
Come here, Cold, and see it rain!

2. Does the title tell you the name of the person who wrote the Hopi prayer? _no_

Thunder strikes and makes it hot.
All seeds grow when it is hot.

3. What kind of weather does the prayer describe? _a thunderstorm; warm weather_

Corn in blossom,
Beans in blossom,
Your face on garden looks,
Watermelon plant, muskmelon plant.
Your face on garden looks.
Aha-aha-ehe-ihe.

4. What season does this poem talk about?
   a. winter
   (b. spring)
   c. summer
5. What is another good title for this poem?
   a. Summer Harvest
   (b. Thunderstorms)
   c. Growing Fruits

Answer Key

A fierce warrior, Crazy Horse was known as a Lakota tribe member who would not give up. Born in 1849, Crazy Horse worked hard to keep the Native American way of life from disappearing. He did not want to lose the customs of his tribe.

1. Turn *would not* into a contraction. __wouldn't__
2. What does *fierce* mean? __tough, won't give up__
3. Why did the author write this paragraph: to tell us about Crazy Horse or to tell us that the Lakota were in danger of losing their customs? __to tell us about Crazy Horse__
4. What did Crazy Horse work hard to do? __keep the Native American way of life from disappearing__

Day #1

Native Americans respect the earth. They (try) to live in harmony with nature. Native Americans use the earth's gifts wisely. These gifts are called natural resources. Natural resources include the land, plants, animals, water, and minerals.

1. Circle the words that end with a *y* that have an **i** sound. Put a line through words that end with a *y* that have an **ee** sound.
2. What does *live in harmony with nature* mean? __to cooperate with nature__
3. What does the author of the paragraph appreciate about Native Americans? __they respect nature and use resources wisely__
4. What are natural resources? __land, plants, animals, minerals__

Day #2

At one time, huge herds of buffalo lived on the plains. The Native Americans followed the buffalo. These people needed the animals for their survival. The animals were used for meat. The hides were used for clothing. The bones were used for tools and jewelry. The tendons were used to string bows.

1. When the author uses the word *live*, is the *i* pronounced like the *i* in the word **hive** or the word **river**? __river__
2. *Hide* is a word that can be used to talk about the skin of an animal. Use *hide* a different way in a sentence. __Let's play hide and seek.__
3. Did Native Americans hunt the buffalo just for fun? __no__
4. What details from the story gave you the answer to #3? __They needed the animals to live.__

Day #3

Wilma Mankiller was born in 1945. She is a Cherokee from Oklahoma. She became principal chief of the Cherokee Nation in 1985. She has worked hard for improved health care and civil rights. Mankiller believes in an old Cherokee saying about being of good mind. She says today this is called "positive thinking."

1. Find a word that is a compound—two words put together to make a new word. __Mankiller__
2. What does *improved* mean? __better__
3. What is another way of saying *positive thinking*? __being of a good mind__
4. What is the author trying to do in this paragraph: **give us information** or **make us laugh**? __give us information__

Day #4

Assessment

Medicine Men and Their Herbs

Did you know Native Americans use plants as medicine? Medicine men use herbs and other plants to help cure illnesses. They gather the plants and dry them to make teas or grind dried herbs into a paste by mixing them with water. They use all parts of the plants in their herbal remedies: the stems, the leaves, the flowers, the bark, and the roots.

If you looked in a medicine man's medicine cabinet you might find garlic cloves for insect stings. Or you might find sunflower seeds and roots to soothe a blister. Slippery elm tea was used for curing sore throats. Dandelion tea was good for heartburn. If you had a problem with dandruff, the medicine man might give you a dose of sword fern tea. He would use pinesap to heal cuts. Witch hazel works on sprains and bruises. He might suggest you chew spruce pine cones for your sore throat. If you couldn't get rid of a headache, he'd probably give you willow bark. Willow bark contains salicyclic acid. That's the main ingredient in aspirin. Many of these herbs are available today in drugstores. You might want to keep some willow bark on hand.

1. What do these words have in common?

   sunflower, heartburn, headache, drugstores

   __They are all compound words—one word made of two words put together.__

2. What is a paste? __a thick mixture of something that was dried and water or another liquid__

3. What part of a sunflower plant can be used to soothe a blister? __seeds and roots__

4. What do you think the author was trying to do in this article?
   - a. tell how medicine men make tea
   - b. (tell how medicine men use plants)
   - c. tell you how to become a medicine man

5. How is willow bark like aspirin? __They both contain salicylic acid, which helps get rid of headaches.__

The Story of the Cherokee Rose

In 1838, the government of the United States made the Cherokees move from their homes in Georgia and other states to what was then called the Indian Territory. That land is now the state of Oklahoma.

1. What clues does the title give us about the subject of this article? __It is a story about something called the Cherokee rose.__
2. Does this paragraph tell us anything about who the Cherokees were? __no__
3. Does this paragraph tell us anything about the rose in the title? __no__
4. How long ago did this story take place? __Answer will vary, depending on the year this work is assigned__

Day #1

The Cherokees had to walk about a thousand miles, and they often did not have enough food or water. Many hundreds of them died. The mothers felt so sad that some of them could not take care of their children.

1. How did the Cherokees get to Indian Territory? __They walked.__
2. Does the author include any opinions in this paragraph? __no__
3. Who is feeling sad in this paragraph? __the Cherokee mothers__
4. This trip is called the Trail of Tears. What clues tell you why? __There was not enough food or water; many people died.__

Day #2

The old men of the tribe asked the Great One for a sign that would make the mothers feel better and make them strong enough to take care of their children.

1. Who in the tribe came up with a solution to the problem? __the old men__
2. What solution did the tribe come up with for the mothers? __They asked the Great One to help the mothers feel better.__
3. Is the Great One **a religious figure** or **the tallest Cherokee**? __a religious figure__
4. If you were the Great One, what kind of sign would you send to make the mothers feel better and be stronger? __Answers will vary.__

Day #3

The Great One promised that where a mother's tear fell, a flower would grow. That flower is called the Cherokee rose. It is white, and that color stands for the mothers' tears. The center of the flower is gold. That is a symbol of the gold that was taken from the tribes' land. The seven leaves on the rose's stem stand for the seven groups of people that walked along the Trail of Tears.

1. Which paragraph told you what the Cherokee rose is? __the last one, in day 4__
2. How does the story say the Cherokee rose comes about? __It grows where a Cherokee mother's tears fall.__
3. What are the different parts of the rose and what are they symbols of? You may want to make a chart. __white-mother's tears; gold-gold taken from the land; seven petals-seven groups of people__
4. How does this story make you feel? __Answers will vary.__

Day #4

Assessment

1. Without looking back on your earlier work, what do you remember about the Trail of Tears? __Answers will vary.__

The Trail of Tears

The ancient Cherokee were hunters and farmers. They lived in the area that we know as the Appalachian Mountains of Georgia. But in 1829, white settlers found gold on this land. They went to the United States government and asked that the Cherokee be forced to leave the land, hoping they would then get the rights to it.

2. Why did the settlers want the Cherokee gone? __The settlers wanted the gold found in the land.__

A new law called the Indian Removal Act of 1830 was passed. The law stated that all Native Americans east of the Mississippi would be moved. They would have to go live on an Indian territory in the west, an area in what is now Oklahoma.

3. Were the settlers successful? __yes__

Some agreed to go, but most would not leave their land. Starting in the spring of 1838, the army gathered the Cherokee together. The people were held in forts like prisoners. Within one month, the first group of Cherokee was forced to leave Georgia. They marched over 1,000 miles to the new land. Some people had horses and wagons. Most people walked. The trip lasted many months. Hundreds died, either during the march or once they got to the land. There was no shelter or food at the territory. The last group of Cherokee arrived on the Indian Territory in March of 1839. In all, almost 17,000 Cherokee were forced to move to the new land.

4. Did the Cherokee go willingly? __no__

5. Which point of view do you agree with: that of the settlers or the Cherokee? Explain your answer. __Answers will vary.__

Answer Key

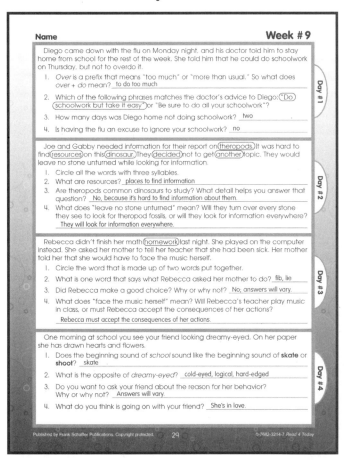

Day #1

Diego came down with the flu on Monday night, and his doctor told him to stay home from school for the rest of the week. She told him that he could do schoolwork on Thursday, but not to overdo it.

1. *Over* is a prefix that means "too much" or "more than usual." So what does *over + do* mean? __to do too much__

2. Which of the following phrases matches the doctor's advice to Diego: "(Do schoolwork but take it easy)" or "Be sure to do all your schoolwork"?

3. How many days was Diego home not doing schoolwork? __two__

4. Is having the flu an excuse to ignore your schoolwork? __no__

Day #2

Joe and Gabby needed information for their report on (theropods). It was hard to find (resources) on this (dinosaur). They (decided) not to get (another) topic. They would leave no stone unturned while looking for information.

1. Circle all the words with three syllables.

2. What are resources? __places to find information__

3. Are theropods common dinosaurs to study? What detail helps you answer that question? __No, because it's hard to find information about them.__

4. What does "leave no stone unturned" mean? Will they turn over every stone they see to look for theropod fossils, or will they look for information everywhere? __They will look for information everywhere.__

Day #3

Rebecca didn't finish her math (homework) last night. She played on the computer instead. She asked her mother to tell her teacher that she had been sick. Her mother told her that she would have to face the music herself.

1. Circle the word that is made up of two words put together.

2. What is one word that says what Rebecca asked her mother to do? __fib, lie__

3. Did Rebecca make a good choice? Why or why not? __No; answers will vary.__

4. What does "face the music herself" mean? Will Rebecca's teacher play music in class, or must Rebecca accept the consequences of her actions? __Rebecca must accept the consequences of her actions.__

Day #4

One morning at school you see your friend looking dreamy-eyed. On her paper she has drawn hearts and flowers.

1. Does the beginning sound of *school* sound like the beginning sound of **skate** or **shoot**? __skate__

2. What is the opposite of *dreamy-eyed*? __cold-eyed, logical, hard-edged__

3. Do you want to ask your friend about the reason for her behavior? Why or why not? __Answers will vary.__

4. What do you think is going on with your friend? __She's in love.__

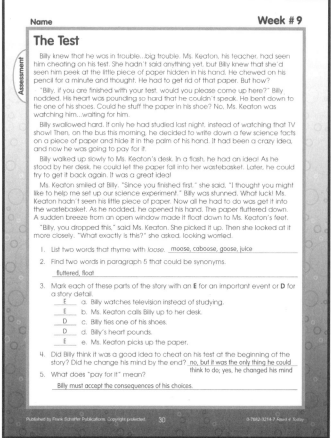

Assessment

The Test

Billy knew that he was in trouble...big trouble. Ms. Keaton, his teacher, had seen him cheating on his test. She hadn't said anything yet, but Billy knew that she'd seen him peek at the little piece of paper hidden in his hand. He chewed on his pencil for a minute and thought. He had to get rid of that paper. But how?

"Billy, if you are finished with your test, would you please come up here?" Billy nodded. His heart was pounding so hard that he couldn't speak. He bent down to tie one of his shoes. Could he stuff the paper in his shoe? No, Ms. Keaton was watching him...waiting for him.

Billy swallowed hard. If only he had studied last night, instead of watching that TV show! Then, on the bus this morning, he decided to write down a few science facts on a piece of paper and hide it in the palm of his hand. It had been a crazy idea, and now he was going to pay for it.

Billy walked up slowly to Ms. Keaton's desk. In a flash, he had an idea! As he stood by her desk, he could let the paper fall into her wastebasket. Later, he could try to get it back again. It was a great idea!

Ms. Keaton smiled at Billy. "Since you finished first," she said, "I thought you might like to help me set up our science experiment." Billy was stunned. What luck! Ms. Keaton hadn't seen his little piece of paper. Now all he had to do was get it into the wastebasket. As he nodded, he opened his hand. The paper fluttered down. A sudden breeze from an open window made it float down to Ms. Keaton's feet.

"Billy, you dropped this," said Ms. Keaton. She picked it up. Then she looked at it more closely. "What exactly is this?" she asked, looking worried.

1. List two words that rhyme with *loose*. __moose, caboose, goose, juice__

2. Find two words in paragraph 5 that could be synonyms. __fluttered, float__

3. Mark each of these parts of the story with an **E** for an important event or **D** for a story detail.
   - __E__ a. Billy watches television instead of studying.
   - __E__ b. Ms. Keaton calls Billy up to her desk.
   - __D__ c. Billy ties one of his shoes.
   - __D__ d. Billy's heart pounds.
   - __E__ e. Ms. Keaton picks up the paper.

4. Did Billy think it was a good idea to cheat on his test at the beginning of the story? Did he change his mind by the end? __no, but it was the only thing he could think to do; yes, he changed his mind__

5. What does "pay for it" mean? __Billy must accept the consequences of his choices.__

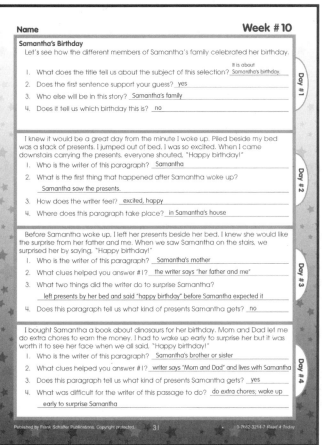

Samantha's Birthday

Let's see how the different members of Samantha's family celebrated her birthday.

Day #1

1. What does the title tell us about the subject of this selection? __It is about Samantha's birthday.__

2. Does the first sentence support your guess? __yes__

3. Who else will be in this story? __Samantha's family__

4. Does it tell us which birthday this is? __no__

Day #2

I knew it would be a great day from the minute I woke up. Piled beside my bed was a stack of presents. I jumped out of bed. I was so excited. When I came downstairs carrying the presents, everyone shouted, "Happy birthday!"

1. Who is the writer of this paragraph? __Samantha__

2. What is the first thing that happened after Samantha woke up? __Samantha saw the presents.__

3. How does the writer feel? __excited, happy__

4. Where does this paragraph take place? __in Samantha's house__

Day #3

Before Samantha woke up, I left her presents beside her bed. I knew she would like the surprise from her father and me. When we saw Samantha on the stairs, we surprised her by saying, "Happy birthday!"

1. Who is the writer of this paragraph? __Samantha's mother__

2. What clues helped you answer #1? __the writer says "her father and me"__

3. What two things did the writer do to surprise Samantha? __left presents by her bed and said "happy birthday" before Samantha expected it__

4. Does this paragraph tell us what kind of presents Samantha gets? __no__

Day #4

I bought Samantha a book about dinosaurs for her birthday. Mom and Dad let me do extra chores to earn the money. I had to wake up early to surprise her but it was worth it to see her face when we all said, "Happy birthday!"

1. Who is the writer of this paragraph? __Samantha's brother or sister__

2. What clues helped you answer #1? __writer says "Mom and Dad" and lives with Samantha__

3. Does this paragraph tell us what kind of presents Samantha gets? __yes__

4. What was difficult for the writer of this passage to do? __do extra chores; wake up early to surprise Samantha__

Assessment

1. Glance down at the reading. What type of writing is it?
   - a. a poem
   - b. religious writings
   - c. (directions)

Putting It All Together

Juanita bought a dinosaur-shaped table as a birthday present for her little brother.

2. What does the first sentence tell us about the main character? __Her name is Juanita, and she bought a dinosaur-shaped table for her little brother.__

The entire table came in a box that was almost flat. Before she started putting the table together, Juanita took out the pieces and read the directions.

3. Have you learned what the title is about? If so, what? __yes, about putting together the table__

Directions:
1. Check to be sure you have all the pieces: one tabletop, four table legs, eight small screws, and four large screws.
2. Snap the table legs into the tabletop holes.
3. Screw in the large screws under the tabletop to hold the legs tight.
4. Screw the small screws into the tabletop where marked.

4. Why is it important for Juanita to be certain that she has all the pieces before she begins to put the table together? __She might be missing a piece and not be able to finish.__

5. Why is it important for directions to list instructions in the correct order? __If the directions are mixed up, so is the project.__

Answer Key

A tarantula is a big, hairy spider. You might have seen one in a pet shop that carries spiders and other unusual pets. In the United States, tarantulas live in the west, where it is hot and dry. During the day, tarantulas sleep in holes and other dark places. They come out at night to hunt for food.

Day #1

1. What word has a *t* that is pronounced like **ch**? _tarantula_
2. Give antonyms for *big, hairy*. _small/tiny/little; bald/just skin/smooth_
3. If you visit a pet shop that carries unusual pets, what pet might you see?
   a. cat   b. canary   (c. tarantula)
4. What might happen if you stuck your hand in a dark hole in Arizona? _You might bother a sleeping tarantula, or a tarantula might bite you._

Tarantulas (catch) their food mostly by jumping on it and biting it. Smaller tarantulas eat insects. Larger ones eat mice and lizards. A tarantula's poison can kill the animals it hunts, but its poison cannot kill a human.

Day #2

1. Circle the word that has an ending sound like the middle *t* in *tarantula*.
2. What is another word for "the animals it hunts"?
   (a. prey)   b. toast   c. pray
3. What information in this paragraph might make you feel better about meeting up with a tarantula? _Its poison can't kill humans._
4. What kills the animals a tarantula hunts? _the poison in its bite_

If you are bitten, you will soon know that a tarantula bite hurts only about as much as a bee sting. Its bite helps this spider protect itself. Tarantulas are shy spiders. They bite humans only if they feel threatened and cannot get away.

Day #3

1. The *i* in *bite* is pronounced a hard i. How is the *i* in *bitten* pronounced? _soft i_
2. What is another word the author could have used instead of *shy*? _timid, afraid_
3. Someone who has been bitten by a tarantula will
   a. jump in the air, dance, and scream.   (b. feel a bite like a bee sting.)
4. Poking or touching a tarantula might make it
   (a. run away.)   b. bite you.   c. run after you until it catches you.

A tarantula has another way to protect itself. It can rub its stiff (hind) legs together, which causes its stiff leg hairs to fly up in the air. Each (tiny) hair can make a hurtful skin or eye wound.

Day #4

1. Circle all the words that have a long *i*.
2. Which meaning of *wound* is correct here: **wrapped around** or (injury)?
3. What details does the writer use to describe tarantula hairs? _stiff, tiny_
4. If you got down on your knees to look closely at a tarantula that was rubbing its hind legs together, what might happen? _The hairs would hurt your skin or eyes._

Assessment

Venus Flytrap

Kayla got a Venus flytrap for her birthday. She put it with her other plants on her windowsill. She watered all of her plants each day.

After a week, all of her plants looked fine except her gift. She decided that she needed more information on this plant, so she went to the library and found a book about the Venus flytrap.

She was surprised to find out that this plant was carnivorous, or meat-eating. No wonder it was not doing well! The book said that the Venus flytrap is a popular house plant. Each set of leaves stays open until an insect or piece of meat lands on the inside of the leaf. The two leaves close quickly, trapping the bait inside. After a leaf digests the meat, it dies. A new leaf grows to take the place of the dead leaf.

Now Kayla knows how to take care of her Venus flytrap.

1. Complete this sentence with a homophone of *week*: After a week the Venus flytrap was _weak_ .
2. What does the word *carnivorous* mean?
   meat-eating
3. What clues from the compound word in the name *Venus flytrap* tell you what it might eat?
   It traps flies, and it eats them.
4. Why did Kayla need to go to the library?
   She needed to find out how to take care of her Venus flytrap.
5. What do you think Kayla will do next?
   Kayla will get some meat for the Venus flytrap to eat.

Special Spiders

Myra watched a bug scamper across the sidewalk. Its little legs moved so quickly.
"That's a cool spider!" said a voice.

Day #1

1. What does the title tell us about the topic of this selection? _It will be about spiders._
2. What is the setting of the story? _the sidewalk outdoors_
3. How does Myra feel about the bug in the sidewalk? _curious, interested_
4. Whose voice do you guess Myra hears: **the spider's** or a **friend's**? _a friend's_

Myra turned around and saw her friend Dave. "How do you know it is a spider?" Myra asked.
"It has eight legs," said Dave. "If you look really closely, you will see that it does not have antennae either."
"When did you get to know so much about spiders?" asked Myra.

Day #2

1. Whose voice did Myra hear? _her friend Dave's_
2. List two characteristics of spiders. _eight legs, no antennae_
3. Is it easy to determine whether there are or are not antennae on a bug? Why or why not? _No; you have to look closely._
4. Would you like to look closely at a bug? Why or why not? _Answers will vary._

"I just read a book about them," Dave answered. "Like insects, spiders are invertebrates. They have a hard outer shell called an exoskeleton. The exoskeleton protects the soft inside parts of their bodies. They also have special eyes that help them hunt. The part I found the most interesting is that the spider, horseshoe crab, and the scorpion all belong to the same group."

Day #3

1. How are insects and spiders similar? _both are invertebrates; special eyes_
2. What did Dave say was the most interesting thing about spiders? _They are in the same group with horseshoe crabs and scorpions._
3. How does Dave feel about spiders? _He likes them and is interested in them._
4. Do you feel the same way? Why or why not? _Answers will vary._

"You have learned so much that I'm surprised you didn't know the name of that spider," said Myra.
"Give me some time," smiled Dave. "I'm reading a book about identifying spiders right now."

Day #4

1. Does Dave know everything there is to know about spiders? _no_
2. What clue helped you answer #1? _He's reading a book about identifying them._
3. How did Dave get his information on spiders? _books_
4. What are some other sources he could go to? _Internet, videos, CD-ROM, zoo_

Assessment

1. What does the title tell you about the subject of this article?
   It will be about insects that are impressive.

Impressive Insects

Periodical cicadas take from 13 to 17 years to change from an egg to a nymph to an adult, and then they live only four to six weeks as an adult. All that work for so little time seems like such a shame.

2. Which sentence in the first paragraph is the author's opinion?
   The last one; "All that work for so little time seems like such a shame."

Green grapplers eat only live insects. They grab an insect with the claws on their six front legs and then eat it. Often their prey is heavier than they are. Could you eat a hamburger that's heavier than you are?

3. If you ate a hamburger that weighed ½ of a pound, how many burgers would you have to eat to eat more than you weigh?
   Answers will vary.

You can't tell if a saddleback caterpillar is coming or going. One end is like the other end. It's symmetrical. It has matched pairs of poisonous horns. One pair is on one end; another pair is on the other end. If you see one coming, or going, don't touch it. It can sting.

4. What is unique about the saddleback caterpillar?
   It is symmetrical.
5. Did the article live up to the title? Which insect do you think is the most impressive?
   Answers will vary.

Answer Key

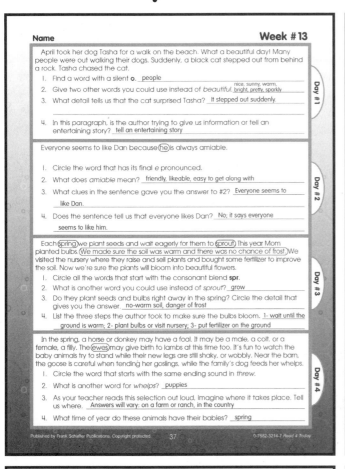

April took her dog Tasha for a walk on the beach. What a beautiful day! Many people were out walking their dogs. Suddenly, a black cat stepped out from behind a rock. Tasha chased the cat.

Day #1

1. Find a word with a silent **o**. __people__
2. Give two other words you could use instead of *beautiful*. __nice, sunny, warm, bright, pretty, sparkly__
3. What detail tells us that the cat surprised Tasha? __It stepped out suddenly.__
4. In this paragraph, is the author trying to give us information or tell an entertaining story? __tell an entertaining story__

Everyone seems to like Dan because (he) is always amiable.

Day #2

1. Circle the word that has its final e pronounced.
2. What does *amiable* mean? __friendly, likeable, easy to get along with__
3. What clues in the sentence gave you the answer to #2? __Everyone seems to like Dan.__
4. Does the sentence tell us that everyone likes Dan? __No; it says everyone seems to like him.__

Each (spring) we plant seeds and wait eagerly for them to (sprout) This year Mom planted bulbs. (We made sure the soil was warm and there was no chance of frost.) We visited the nursery where they raise and sell plants and bought some fertilizer to improve the soil. Now we're sure the plants will bloom into beautiful flowers.

Day #3

1. Circle all the words that start with the consonant blend **spr**.
2. What is another word you could use instead of *sprout*? __grow__
3. Do they plant seeds and bulbs right away in the spring? Circle the detail that gives you the answer. __no-warm soil, danger of frost__
4. List the three steps the author took to make sure the bulbs bloom. __1- wait until the ground is warm; 2- plant bulbs or visit nursery; 3- put fertilizer on the ground__

In the spring, a horse or donkey may have a foal. It may be a male, a colt, or a female, a filly. (ewes) may give birth to lambs at this time too. It's fun to watch the baby animals try to stand while their new legs are still shaky, or wobbly. Near the barn, the goose is careful when tending her goslings, while the family's dog feeds her whelps.

Day #4

1. Circle the word that starts with the same ending sound in *threw*.
2. What is another word for *whelps*? __puppies__
3. As your teacher reads this selection out loud, imagine where it takes place. Tell us where. __Answers will vary: on a farm or ranch, in the country__
4. What time of year do these animals have their babies? __spring__

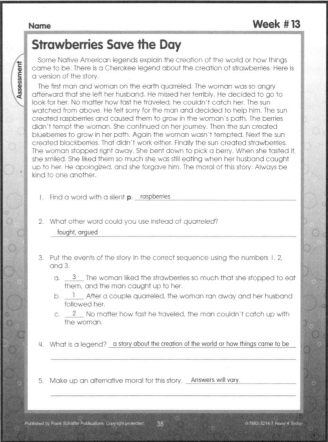

Assessment

Strawberries Save the Day

Some Native American legends explain the creation of the world or how things came to be. There is a Cherokee legend about the creation of strawberries. Here is a version of the story.

The first man and woman on the earth quarreled. The woman was so angry afterward that she left her husband. He missed her terribly. He decided to go to look for her. No matter how fast he traveled, he couldn't catch her. The sun watched from above. He felt sorry for the man and decided to help him. The sun created raspberries and caused them to grow in the woman's path. The berries didn't tempt the woman. She continued on her journey. Then the sun created blueberries to grow in her path. Again the woman wasn't tempted. Next the sun created blackberries. That didn't work either. Finally the sun created strawberries. The woman stopped right away. She bent down to pick a berry. When she tasted it, she smiled. She liked them so much she was still eating when her husband caught up to her. He apologized, and she forgave him. The moral of this story: Always be kind to one another.

1. Find a word with a silent **p**. __raspberries__
2. What other word could you use instead of *quarreled*? __fought, argued__
3. Put the events of the story in the correct sequence using the numbers 1, 2, and 3.
   a. __3__ The woman liked the strawberries so much that she stopped to eat them, and the man caught up to her.
   b. __1__ After a couple quarreled, the woman ran away and her husband followed her.
   c. __2__ No matter how fast he traveled, the man couldn't catch up with the woman.
4. What is a legend? __a story about the creation of the world or how things came to be__
5. Make up an alternative moral for this story. __Answers will vary.__

Lazy Time
Sally and Ned are swaying slowly in the family swing.

Day #1

1. What does the title tell us about the story? __It will be about a lazy time.__
2. What information does the opening sentence add? __Ned and Sally are in a swing.__
3. Is there an image in the first sentence that supports or illustrates the title? __yes__
4. If so, what is it and how does it illustrate the title? __They sway slowly. If it weren't a lazy time, they'd swing fast or not be in a swing.__

The air is crisp. Sally puts her arm around Ned and snuggles into his shaggy body. Ned's tongue licks Sally's hand that lies on her blue-jeaned leg. They watch a sluggish ladybug crawl underneath a pile of old, brown leaves. One red leaf drifts to the top of the ladybug's leaf pile.

Day #2

1. What time of year is it? __fall or autumn__
2. What clues helped you answer #1? __The air is crisp, and leaves are falling.__
3. What or who do you think Ned is? __a dog__
4. What clues helped you answer #3? __His body is shaggy; he licks Sally's hand.__

Ned's graying ears prick up as a southbound V of geese honks goodbye. The sky slowly turns from blue, to pink, to purple, to black.
The first star shines as Sally's mom calls her in to eat. Sally gives a last push as she slides out of the swing. She walks to the back door of the house. Ned leaps down.

Day #3

1. What sounds can you hear in this selection? __geese honking, mom calling__
2. Is Ned a puppy or an older dog? __an older dog__
3. What clues helped you answer #2? __His ears are graying.__
4. How does Sally feel? __happy__

Ned barks once at a rabbit, and then chases after Sally. She smiles and rubs Ned's head as they walk into the warm house together.

Day #4

1. What meal is Sally about to eat? __dinner__
2. Did the title set up the story well? __yes__
3. List the words in all the selections that give a picture of laziness. __swaying slowly, sluggish, drifts, slowly turns, walks__
4. What other title would work? __Answers will vary.__

Assessment

1. This is a table of contents for a book. What does a table of contents tell you? __the names of chapters in a book and what pages to find them on__

A Year in My Life

CONTENTS

2. What time of year is it in the first three chapters? __late summer and fall__

3. What season is it in chapters 7-9? __spring__

4. Do you think chapter 13 is about the harvest festival of Thanksgiving or about the author harvesting food from a garden? What clues helped you answer that question? __The author is harvesting food, because there's already a chapter about Thanksgiving (3), and in chapter 11, the author tends a garden.__
5. Is the book arranged thematically (by theme) or chronologically (by time)? __chronologically__

Answer Key

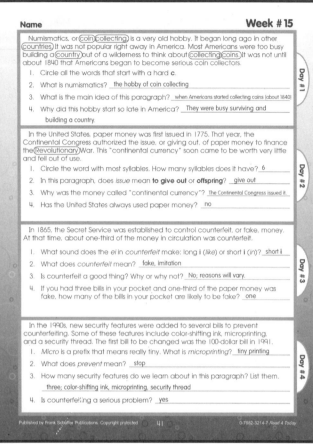

Numismatics, or (coin)(collecting,) is a very old hobby. It began long ago in other (countries.) It was not popular right away in America. Most Americans were too busy building a (country) out of a wilderness to think about (collecting)(coins.) It was not until about 1840 that Americans began to become serious coin collectors.

Day #1

1. Circle all the words that start with a hard **c**.
2. What is numismatics? _the hobby of coin collecting_
3. What is the main idea of this paragraph? _when Americans started collecting coins (about 1840)_
4. Why did this hobby start so late in America? _They were busy surviving and building a country._

In the United States, paper money was first issued in 1775. That year, the Continental Congress authorized the issue, or giving out, of paper money to finance the (Revolutionary) War. This "continental currency" soon came to be worth very little and fell out of use.

Day #2

1. Circle the word with most syllables. How many syllables does it have? _6_
2. In this paragraph, does *issue* mean **to give out** or **offspring**? _give out_
3. Why was the money called "continental currency"? _The Continental Congress issued it._
4. Has the United States always used paper money? _no_

In 1865, the Secret Service was established to control counterfeit, or fake, money. At that time, about one-third of the money in circulation was counterfeit.

Day #3

1. What sound does the *ei* in *counterfeit* make: long **i** (*like*) or short **i** (*in*)? _short i_
2. What does *counterfeit* mean? _fake, imitation_
3. Is counterfeit a good thing? Why or why not? _No; reasons will vary._
4. If you had three bills in your pocket and one-third of the paper money was fake, how many of the bills in your pocket are likely to be fake? _one_

In the 1990s, new security features were added to several bills to prevent counterfeiting. Some of these features include color-shifting ink, microprinting, and a security thread. The first bill to be changed was the 100-dollar bill in 1991.

Day #4

1. *Micro* is a prefix that means really tiny. What is *microprinting*? _tiny printing_
2. What does *prevent* mean? _stop_
3. How many security features do we learn about in this paragraph? List them. _three; color-shifting ink, microprinting, security thread_
4. Is counterfeiting a serious problem? _yes_

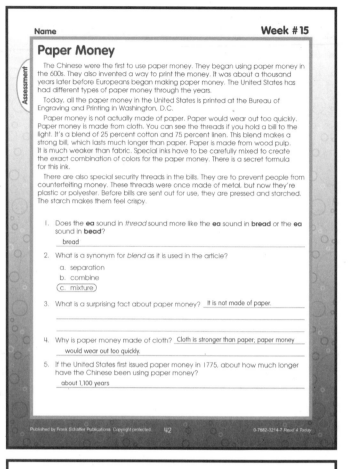

Assessment

Paper Money

The Chinese were the first to use paper money. They began using paper money in the 600s. They also invented a way to print the money. It was about a thousand years later before Europeans began making paper money. The United States has had different types of paper money through the years.

Today, all the paper money in the United States is printed at the Bureau of Engraving and Printing in Washington, D.C.

Paper money is not actually made of paper. Paper would wear out too quickly. Paper money is made from cloth. You can see the threads if you hold a bill to the light. It's a blend of 25 percent cotton and 75 percent linen. This blend makes a strong bill, which lasts much longer than paper. Paper is made from wood pulp. It is much weaker than fabric. Special inks have to be carefully mixed to create the exact combination of colors for the paper money. There is a secret formula for this ink.

There are also special security threads in the bills. They are to prevent people from counterfeiting money. These threads were once made of metal, but now they're plastic or polyester. Before bills are sent out for use, they are pressed and starched. The starch makes them feel crispy.

1. Does the **ea** sound in *thread* sound more like the **ea** sound in **bread** or the **ea** sound in **bead**?
   bread

2. What is a synonym for *blend* as it is used in the article?
   a. separation
   b. combine
   c. mixture

3. What is a surprising fact about paper money? _It is not made of paper._

4. Why is paper money made of cloth? _Cloth is stronger than paper; paper money would wear out too quickly._

5. If the United States first issued paper money in 1775, about how much longer have the Chinese been using paper money?
   about 1,100 years

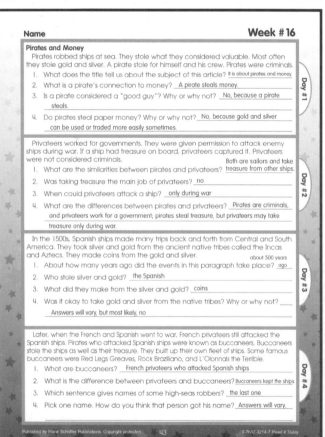

Pirates and Money

Pirates robbed ships at sea. They stole what they considered valuable. Most often they stole gold and silver. A pirate stole for himself and his crew. Pirates were criminals.

Day #1

1. What does the title tell us about the subject of this article? _It is about pirates and money._
2. What is a pirate's connection to money? _A pirate steals money._
3. Is a pirate considered a "good guy"? Why or why not? _No, because a pirate steals._
4. Do pirates steal paper money? Why or why not? _No, because gold and silver can be used or traded more easily sometimes._

Privateers worked for governments. They were given permission to attack enemy ships during war. If a ship had treasure on board, privateers captured it. Privateers were not considered criminals.

Day #2

1. What are the similarities between pirates and privateers? _Both are sailors and take treasure from other ships._
2. Was taking treasure the main job of privateers? _no_
3. When could privateers attack a ship? _only during war_
4. What are the differences between pirates and privateers? _Pirates are criminals, and privateers work for a government; pirates steal treasure, but privateers may take treasure only during war._

In the 1500s, Spanish ships made many trips back and forth from Central and South America. They took silver and gold from the ancient native tribes called the Incas and Aztecs. They made coins from the gold and silver.

Day #3

1. About how many years ago did the events in this paragraph take place? _about 500 years ago_
2. Who stole silver and gold? _the Spanish_
3. What did they make from the silver and gold? _coins_
4. Was it okay to take gold and silver from the native tribes? Why or why not? _Answers will vary, but most likely, no_

Later, when the French and Spanish went to war, French privateers still attacked the Spanish ships. Pirates who attacked Spanish ships were known as buccaneers. Buccaneers stole the ships as well as their treasure. They built up their own fleet of ships. Some famous buccaneers were Red Legs Greaves, Rock Braziliano, and L'Olonnais the Terrible.

Day #4

1. What are buccaneers? _French privateers who attacked Spanish ships_
2. What is the difference between privateers and buccaneers? _Buccaneers kept the ships_
3. Which sentence gives names of some high-seas robbers? _the last one_
4. Pick one name. How do you think that person got his name? _Answers will vary._

Assessment

1. Look at the title. How do you think this selection will be different from the earlier selection on pirates?
   This selection will be about individual pirates.

Famous Pirates

Captain Kidd was a famous pirate. His real name was William Kidd. He was a seaman. He was hired to search for pirates. He worked as a privateer in England but began stealing for himself. He and his crew attacked the *Quedah Merchant*. They stole gold bars and coins worth about $93,000. They also stole the ship. Kidd was convicted of piracy and hanged in 1701. Some of his treasure was found in Long Island, New York. Some people believe there is more to be found.

2. How did Captain Kidd become a pirate? _He was a privateer but began stealing for himself._

Another famous pirate was Blackbeard. His real name was Edward Teach. He twisted his long black beard into long pigtails. In his belt he carried daggers, pistols, and a cutlass, which is a short, heavy sword with a curved blade. He terrified his enemies.

3. What made Blackbeard famous? _his long black beard, how scared his enemies were of him_

The British and American navies put a stop to most piracy at the end of the eighteenth century. However, there are still some pirates working today. Today's pirates have guns instead of swords.

4. Is being a pirate a safe lifestyle? Use clues from the entire article to help you answer that question.
   No; Captain Kidd was hanged, and Blackbeard always carried many weapons.

5. Which do you think is a more effective weapon for a pirate: a gun or a sword? Why?
   Answers will vary, but probably a gun, because it can be used it from a greater distance.

Answer Key

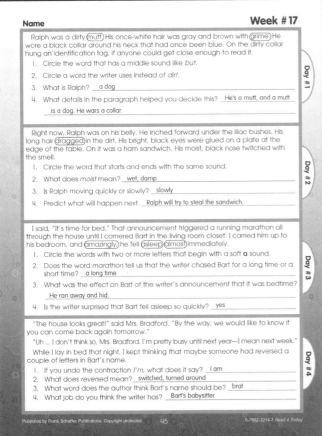

Week # 17

Ralph was a dirty (mutt) His once-white hair was gray and brown with (grime) He wore a black collar around his neck that had once been blue. On the dirty collar hung an identification tag, if anyone could get close enough to read it.

Day #1

1. Circle the word that has a middle sound like *but*.
2. Circle a word the writer uses instead of *dirt*.
3. What is Ralph? __a dog__
4. What details in the paragraph helped you decide this? __He's a mutt, and a mutt is a dog. He wears a collar.__

Right now, Ralph was on his belly. He inched forward under the lilac bushes. His long hair (dragged) in the dirt. His bright, black eyes were glued on a plate at the edge of the table. On it was a ham sandwich. His moist, black nose twitched with the smell.

Day #2

1. Circle the word that starts and ends with the same sound.
2. What does *moist* mean? __wet, damp__
3. Is Ralph moving quickly or slowly? __slowly__
4. Predict what will happen next. __Ralph will try to steal the sandwich.__

I said, "It's time for bed." That announcement triggered a running marathon all through the house until I cornered Bart in the living room closet. All morning long, we sit carried him up to his bedroom, and (amazingly) he fell (asleep) (almost) immediately.

Day #3

1. Circle the words with two or more letters that begin with a soft **a** sound.
2. Does the word *marathon* tell us that the writer chased Bart for a long time or a short time? __a long time__
3. What was the effect on Bart of the writer's announcement that it was bedtime? __He ran away and hid.__
4. Is the writer surprised that Bart fell asleep so quickly? __yes__

"The house looks great!" said Mrs. Bradford. "By the way, we would like to know if you can come back again tomorrow."
"Uh ... I don't think so, Mrs. Bradford. I'm pretty busy until next year—I mean next week."
While I lay in bed that night, I kept thinking that maybe someone had reversed a couple of letters in Bart's name.

Day #4

1. If you undo the contraction *I'm*, what does it say? __I am__
2. What does *reversed* mean? __switched, turned around__
3. What word does the author think Bart's name should be? __brat__
4. What job do you think the writer has? __Bart's babysitter__

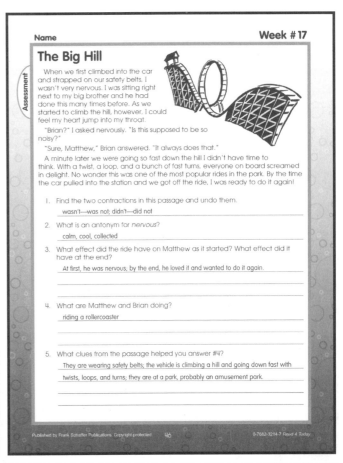

Week # 17

Assessment

The Big Hill

When we first climbed into the car and strapped on our safety belts, I wasn't very nervous. I was sitting right next to my big brother and he had done this many times before. As we started to climb the hill, however, I could feel my heart jump into my throat.

"Brian?" I asked nervously. "Is this supposed to be so noisy?"

"Sure, Matthew," Brian answered. "It always does that."

A minute later we were going so fast down the hill I didn't have time to think. With a twist, a loop, and a bunch of fast turns, everyone on board screamed in delight. No wonder this was one of the most popular rides in the park. By the time the car pulled into the station and we got off the ride, I was ready to do it again!

1. Find the two contractions in this passage and undo them.
   __wasn't—was not; didn't—did not__
2. What is an antonym for *nervous*?
   __calm, cool, collected__
3. What effect did the ride have on Matthew as it started? What effect did it have at the end?
   __At first, he was nervous; by the end, he loved it and wanted to do it again.__
4. What are Matthew and Brian doing?
   __riding a rollercoaster__
5. What clues from the passage helped you answer #4?
   __They are wearing safety belts; the vehicle is climbing a hill and going down fast with twists, loops, and turns; they are at a park, probably an amusement park.__

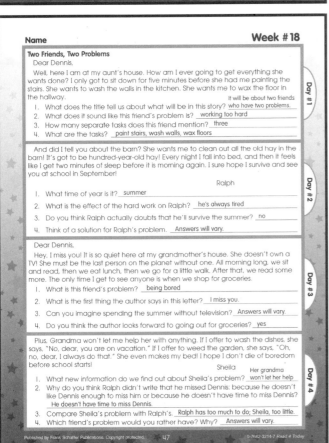

Week # 18

Two Friends, Two Problems

Dear Dennis,
Well, here I am at my aunt's house. How am I ever going to get everything she wants done? I only got to sit down for five minutes before she had me painting the stairs. She wants to wash the walls in the kitchen. She wants me to wax the floor in the hallway.

Day #1

1. What does the title tell us about what will be in this story? __who have two problems.__ (It will be about two friends)
2. What does it sound like this friend's problem is? __working too hard__
3. How many separate tasks does this friend mention? __three__
4. What are the tasks? __paint stairs, wash walls, wax floors__

And did I tell you about the barn? She wants me to clean out all the old hay in the barn! It's got to be hundred-year-old hay! Every night I fall into bed, and then it feels like I get two minutes of sleep before it is morning again. I sure hope I survive and see you at school in September!
Ralph

Day #2

1. What time of year is it? __summer__
2. What is the effect of the hard work on Ralph? __he's always tired__
3. Do you think Ralph actually doubts that he'll survive the summer? __no__
4. Think of a solution for Ralph's problem. __Answers will vary.__

Dear Dennis,
Hey, I miss you! It is so quiet here at my grandmother's house. She doesn't own a TV! She must be the last person on the planet without one. All morning long, we sit and read, then we eat lunch, then we go for a little walk. After that, we read some more. The only time I get to see anyone is when we shop for groceries.

Day #3

1. What is this friend's problem? __being bored__
2. What is the first thing she says in this letter? __I miss you.__
3. Can you imagine spending the summer without television? __Answers will vary.__
4. Do you think the author looks forward to going out for groceries? __yes__

Plus, Grandma won't let me help her with anything. If I offer to wash the dishes, she says, "No, dear, you are on vacation." If I offer to weed the garden, she says, "Oh, no, dear, I always do that." She even makes my bed! I hope I don't die of boredom before school starts!
Sheila

Day #4

1. What new information do we find out about Sheila's problem? __Her grandma won't let her help__
2. Why do you think Ralph didn't write that he missed Dennis: because he doesn't like Dennis enough to miss him or because he doesn't have time to miss Dennis? __He doesn't have time to miss Dennis.__
3. Compare Sheila's problem with Ralph's. __Ralph has too much to do; Sheila, too little.__
4. Which friend's problem would you rather have? Why? __Answers will vary.__

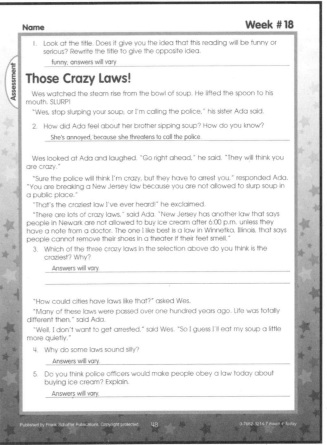

Week # 18

Assessment

1. Look at the title. Does it give you the idea that this reading will be funny or serious? Rewrite the title to give the opposite idea.
   __funny; answers will vary__

Those Crazy Laws!

Wes watched the steam rise from the bowl of soup. He lifted the spoon to his mouth. SLURP!

"Wes, stop slurping your soup, or I'm calling the police," his sister Ada said.

2. How did Ada feel about her brother sipping soup? How do you know?
   __She's annoyed, because she threatens to call the police.__

Wes looked at Ada and laughed. "Go right ahead," he said. "They will think you are crazy."

"Sure the police will think I'm crazy, but they have to arrest you," responded Ada. "You are breaking a New Jersey law because you are not allowed to slurp soup in a public place."

"That's the craziest law I've ever heard!" he exclaimed.

"There are lots of crazy laws," said Ada. "New Jersey has another law that says people in Newark are not allowed to buy ice cream after 6:00 p.m. unless they have a note from a doctor. The one I like best is a law in Winnetka, Illinois, that says people cannot remove their shoes in a theater if their feet smell."

3. Which of the three crazy laws in the selection above do you think is the craziest? Why?
   __Answers will vary.__

"How could cities have laws like that?" asked Wes.

"Many of these laws were passed over one hundred years ago. Life was totally different then," said Ada.

"Well, I don't want to get arrested," said Wes. "So I guess I'll eat my soup a little more quietly."

4. Why do some laws sound silly?
   __Answers will vary.__
5. Do you think police officers would make people obey a law today about buying ice cream? Explain.
   __Answers will vary.__

Answer Key

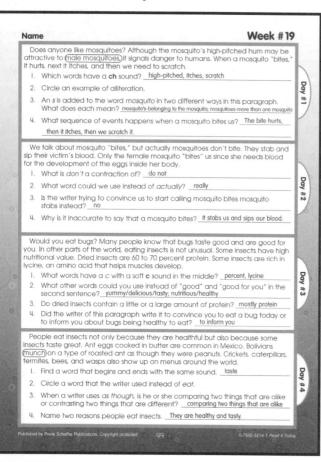

Day #1

Does anyone like mosquitoes? Although the mosquito's high-pitched hum may be attractive to (male mosquitoes,) it signals danger to humans. When a mosquito "bites," it hurts, next it itches, and then we need to scratch.

1. Which words have a **ch** sound? _high-pitched, itches, scratch_

2. Circle an example of alliteration.

3. An *s* is added to the word *mosquito* in two different ways in this paragraph. What does each mean? _mosquito's-belonging to the mosquito; mosquitoes-more than one mosquito_

4. What sequence of events happens when a mosquito bites us? _The bite hurts, then it itches, then we scratch it._

Day #2

We talk about mosquito "bites," but actually mosquitoes don't bite. They stab and sip their victim's blood. Only the female mosquito "bites" us since she needs blood for the development of the eggs inside her body.

1. What is *don't* a contraction of? _do not_

2. What word could we use instead of *actually*? _really_

3. Is the writer trying to convince us to start calling mosquito bites mosquito stabs instead? _no_

4. Why is it inaccurate to say that a mosquito bites? _It stabs us and sips our blood._

Day #3

Would you eat bugs? Many people know that bugs taste good and are good for you. In other parts of the world, eating insects is not unusual. Some insects have high nutritional value. Dried insects are 60 to 70 percent protein. Some insects are rich in lycine, an amino acid that helps muscles develop.

1. What words have a *c* with a soft **c** sound in the middle? _percent, lycine_

2. What other words could you use instead of "good" and "good for you" in the second sentence? _yummy/delicious/tasty; nutritious/healthy_

3. Do dried insects contain a little or a large amount of protein? _mostly protein_

4. Did the writer of this paragraph write it to convince you to eat a bug today or to inform you about bugs being healthy to eat? _to inform you_

Day #4

People eat insects not only because they are healthful but also because some insects taste great. Ant eggs cooked in butter are common in Mexico. Bolivians (munch) on a type of roasted ant as though they were peanuts. Crickets, caterpillars, termites, bees, and wasps also show up on menus around the world.

1. Find a word that begins and ends with the same sound. _taste_

2. Circle a word that the writer used instead of *eat*.

3. When a writer uses *as though*, is he or she comparing two things that are alike or contrasting two things that are different? _comparing two things that are alike_

4. Name two reasons people eat insects. _They are healthy and tasty._

Published by Frank Schaffer Publications. Copyright protected.   49   0-7682-3214-7 *Read 4 Today*

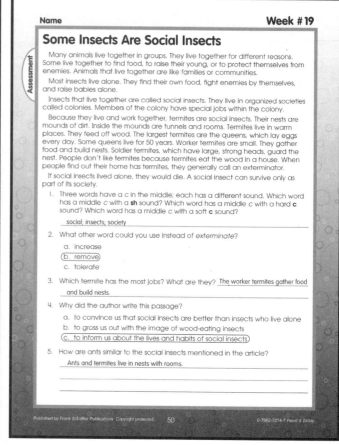

Assessment

Some Insects Are Social Insects

Many animals live together in groups. They live together for different reasons. Some live together to find food, to raise their young, or to protect themselves from enemies. Animals that live together are like families or communities.

Most insects live alone. They find their own food, fight enemies by themselves, and raise babies alone.

Insects that live together are called social insects. They live in organized societies called colonies. Members of the colony have special jobs within the colony.

Because they live and work together, termites are social insects. Their nests are mounds of dirt. Inside the mounds are tunnels and rooms. Termites live in warm places. They feed off wood. The largest termites are the queens, which lay eggs every day. Some queens live for 50 years. Worker termites are small. They gather food and build nests. Soldier termites, which have large, strong heads, guard the nest. People don't like termites because termites eat the wood in a house. When people find out their home has termites, they generally call an exterminator.

If social insects lived alone, they would die. A social insect can survive only as part of its society.

1. Three words have a *c* in the middle; each has a different sound. Which word has a middle *c* with a **sh** sound? Which word has a middle *c* with a hard **c** sound? Which word has a middle *c* with a soft **c** sound?
   social; insects; society

2. What other word could you use instead of *exterminate*?
   a. increase
   b. (remove)
   c. tolerate

3. Which termite has the most jobs? What are they? _The worker termites gather food and build nests._

4. Why did the author write this passage?
   a. to convince us that social insects are better than insects who live alone
   b. to gross us out with the image of wood-eating insects
   c. (to inform us about the lives and habits of social insects)

5. How are ants similar to the social insects mentioned in the article? _Ants and termites live in nests with rooms._

Published by Frank Schaffer Publications. Copyright protected.   50   0-7682-3214-7 *Read 4 Today*

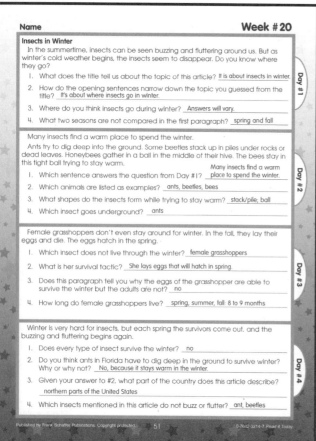

Insects in Winter

In the summertime, insects can be seen buzzing and fluttering around us. But as winter's cold weather begins, the insects seem to disappear. Do you know where they go?

Day #1

1. What does the title tell us about the topic of this article? _It is about insects in winter._

2. How do the opening sentences narrow down the topic you guessed from the title? _It's about where insects go in winter._

3. Where do you think insects go during winter? _Answers will vary._

4. What two seasons are not compared in the first paragraph? _spring and fall_

Many insects find a warm place to spend the winter.

Ants try to dig deep into the ground. Some beetles stack up in piles under rocks or dead leaves. Honeybees gather in a ball in the middle of their hive. The bees stay in this tight ball trying to stay warm.

Day #2

1. Which sentence answers the question from Day #1? _Many insects find a warm place to spend the winter._

2. Which animals are listed as examples? _ants, beetles, bees_

3. What shapes do the insects form while trying to stay warm? _stack/pile; ball_

4. Which insect goes underground? _ants_

Female grasshoppers don't even stay around for winter. In the fall, they lay their eggs and die. The eggs hatch in the spring.

Day #3

1. Which insect does not live through the winter? _female grasshoppers_

2. What is her survival tactic? _She lays eggs that will hatch in spring._

3. Does this paragraph tell you that the eggs of the grasshopper are able to survive the winter but the adults are not? _no_

4. How long do female grasshoppers live? _spring, summer, fall: 8 to 9 months_

Winter is very hard for insects, but each spring the survivors come out, and the buzzing and fluttering begins again.

Day #4

1. Does every type of insect survive the winter? _no_

2. Do you think ants in Florida have to dig deep in the ground to survive winter? Why or why not? _No, because it stays warm in the winter._

3. Given your answer to #2, what part of the country does this article describe? _northern parts of the United States_

4. Which insects mentioned in this article do not buzz or flutter? _ant, beetles_

Published by Frank Schaffer Publications. Copyright protected.   51   0-7682-3214-7 *Read 4 Today*

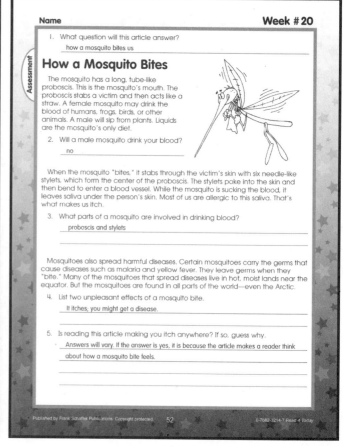

Assessment

1. What question will this article answer? _how a mosquito bites us_

How a Mosquito Bites

The mosquito has a long, tube-like proboscis. This is the mosquito's mouth. The proboscis stabs a victim and then acts like a straw. A female mosquito may drink the blood of humans, frogs, birds, or other animals. A male will sip from plants. Liquids are the mosquito's only diet.

2. Will a male mosquito drink your blood? _no_

When the mosquito "bites," it stabs through the victim's skin with six needle-like stylets, which form the center of the proboscis. The stylets poke into the skin and then bend to enter a blood vessel. While the mosquito is sucking the blood, it leaves saliva under the person's skin. Most of us are allergic to this saliva. That's what makes us itch.

3. What parts of a mosquito are involved in drinking blood? _proboscis and stylets_

Mosquitoes also spread harmful diseases. Certain mosquitoes carry the germs that cause diseases such as malaria and yellow fever. They leave germs when they "bite." Many of the mosquitoes that spread diseases live in hot, moist lands near the equator. But the mosquitoes are found in all parts of the world—even the Arctic.

4. List two unpleasant effects of a mosquito bite. _It itches; you might get a disease._

5. Is reading this article making you itch anywhere? If so, guess why. _Answers will vary. If the answer is yes, it is because the article makes a reader think about how a mosquito bite feels._

Published by Frank Schaffer Publications. Copyright protected.   52   0-7682-3214-7 *Read 4 Today*

Answer Key

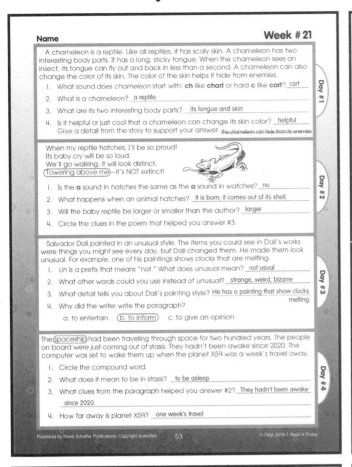

Week # 21

Name

Day #1

A chameleon is a reptile. Like all reptiles, it has scaly skin. A chameleon has two interesting body parts. It has a long, sticky tongue. When the chameleon sees an insect, its tongue can fly out and back in less than a second. A chameleon can also change the color of its skin. The color of the skin helps it hide from enemies.

1. What sound does *chameleon* start with: **ch** like **chart** or hard **c** like **cart**? _cart_

2. What is a chameleon? _a reptile_

3. What are its two interesting body parts? _its tongue and skin_

4. Is it helpful or just cool that a chameleon can change its skin color? _helpful_
   Give a detail from the story to support your answer. _The chameleon can hide from its enemies._

Day #2

When my reptile hatches, I'll be so proud!
Its baby cry will be so loud.
We'll go walking, it will look distinct,
(Towering above me)—it's NOT extinct!

1. Is the **a** sound in *hatches* the same as the **a** sound in *watches*? _no_

2. What happens when an animal hatches? _It is born; it comes out of its shell._

3. Will the baby reptile be larger or smaller than the author? _larger_

4. Circle the clues in the poem that helped you answer #3.

Day #3

Salvador Dali painted in an unusual style. The items you could see in Dali's works were things you might see every day, but Dali changed them. He made them look unusual. For example, one of his paintings shows clocks that are melting.

1. *Un* is a prefix that means "not." What does *unusual* mean? _not usual_

2. What other words could you use instead of *unusual*? _strange, weird, bizarre_

3. What detail tells you about Dali's painting style? _He has a painting that show clocks melting._

4. Why did the writer write the paragraph?
   a. to entertain   (b. to inform)   c. to give an opinion

Day #4

The (spaceship) had been traveling through space for two hundred years. The people on board were just coming out of stasis. They hadn't been awake since 2020. The computer was set to wake them up when the planet X59 was a week's travel away.

1. Circle the compound word.

2. What does it mean to be in stasis? _to be asleep_

3. What clues from the paragraph helped you answer #2? _They hadn't been awake since 2020._

4. How far away is planet X59? _one week's travel_

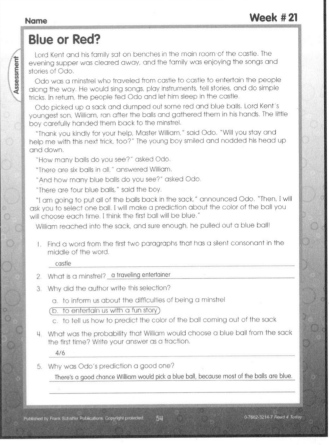

Week # 21

Name

Assessment

Blue or Red?

Lord Kent and his family sat on benches in the main room of the castle. The evening supper was cleared away, and the family was enjoying the songs and stories of Odo.

Odo was a minstrel who traveled from castle to castle to entertain the people along the way. He would sing songs, play instruments, tell stories, and do simple tricks. In return, the people fed Odo and let him sleep in the castle.

Odo picked up a sack and dumped out some red and blue balls. Lord Kent's youngest son, William, ran after the balls and gathered them in his hands. The little boy carefully handed them back to the minstrel.

"Thank you kindly for your help, Master William," said Odo. "Will you stay and help me with this next trick, too?" The young boy smiled and nodded his head up and down.

"How many balls do you see?" asked Odo.

"There are six balls in all," answered William.

"And how many blue balls do you see?" asked Odo.

"There are four blue balls," said the boy.

"I am going to put all of the balls back in the sack," announced Odo. "Then, I will ask you to select one ball. I will make a prediction about the color of the ball you will choose each time. I think the first ball will be blue."

William reached into the sack, and sure enough, he pulled out a blue ball!

1. Find a word from the first two paragraphs that has a silent consonant in the middle of the word.
   castle

2. What is a minstrel? _a traveling entertainer_

3. Why did the author write this selection?
   a. to inform us about the difficulties of being a minstrel
   (b. to entertain us with a fun story)
   c. to tell us how to predict the color of the ball coming out of the sack

4. What was the probability that William would choose a blue ball from the sack the first time? Write your answer as a fraction.
   _4/6_

5. Why was Odo's prediction a good one?
   There's a good chance William would pick a blue ball, because most of the balls are blue.

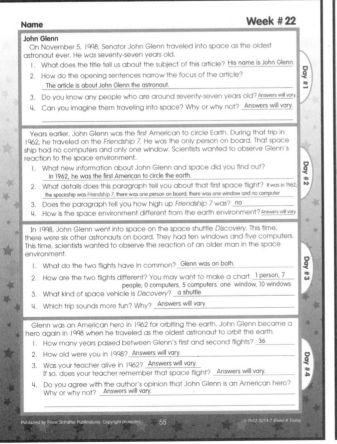

Week # 22

Name

Day #1

John Glenn

On November 5, 1998, Senator John Glenn traveled into space as the oldest astronaut ever. He was seventy-seven years old.

1. What does the title tell us about the subject of this article? _His name is John Glenn_

2. How do the opening sentences narrow the focus of the article?
   The article is about John Glenn the astronaut.

3. Do you know any people who are around seventy-seven years old? _Answers will vary._

4. Can you imagine them traveling into space? Why or why not? _Answers will vary._

Day #2

Years earlier, John Glenn was the first American to circle Earth. During that trip in 1962, he traveled on the *Friendship 7*. He was the only person on board. That space ship had no computers and only one window. Scientists wanted to observe Glenn's reaction to the space environment.

1. What new information about John Glenn and space did you find out? _In 1962, he was the first American to circle the earth._

2. What details does this paragraph tell you about that first space flight? _It was in 1962; the spaceship was Friendship 7; there was one person on board; there was one window and no computer_

3. Does the paragraph tell you how high up *Friendship 7* was? _no_

4. How is the space environment different from the earth environment? _Answers will vary_

Day #3

In 1998, John Glenn went into space on the space shuttle *Discovery*. This time, there were six other astronauts on board. They had ten windows and five computers. This time, scientists wanted to observe the reaction of an older man in the space environment.

1. What do the two flights have in common? _Glenn was on both._

2. How are the two flights different? You may want to make a chart. _1 person, 7 people; 0 computers, 5 computers, one window, 10 windows_

3. What kind of space vehicle is *Discovery*? _a shuttle_

4. Which trip sounds more fun? Why? _Answers will vary._

Day #4

Glenn was an American hero in 1962 for orbiting the earth. John Glenn became a hero again in 1998 when he traveled as the oldest astronaut to orbit the earth.

1. How many years passed between Glenn's first and second flights? _36_

2. How old were you in 1998? _Answers will vary._

3. Was your teacher alive in 1962? _Answers will vary._
   If so, does your teacher remember that space flight? _Answers will vary._

4. Do you agree with the author's opinion that John Glenn is an American hero? Why or why not? _Answers will vary._

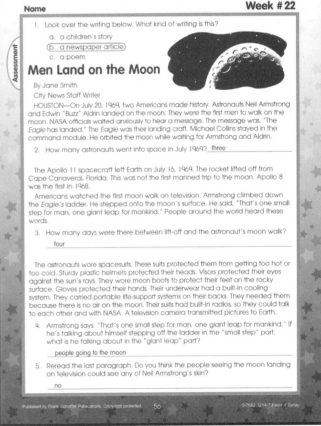

Week # 22

Name

Assessment

1. Look over the writing below. What kind of writing is this?
   a. a children's story
   (b. a newspaper article)
   c. a poem

Men Land on the Moon

By Jane Smith
City News Staff Writer

HOUSTON—On July 20, 1969, two Americans made history. Astronauts Neil Armstrong and Edwin "Buzz" Aldrin landed on the moon. They were the first men to walk on the moon. NASA officials waited anxiously to hear a message. The message was, "The *Eagle* has landed." The *Eagle* was their landing craft. Michael Collins stayed in the command module. He orbited the moon while waiting for Armstrong and Aldrin.

2. How many astronauts went into space in July 1969? _three_

The Apollo 11 spacecraft left Earth on July 16, 1969. The rocket lifted off from Cape Canaveral, Florida. This was not the first manned trip to the moon. Apollo 8 was the first in 1968.

Americans watched the first moon walk on television. Armstrong climbed down the *Eagle's* ladder. He stepped onto the moon's surface. He said, "That's one small step for man, one giant leap for mankind." People around the world heard these words.

3. How many days were there between lift-off and the astronaut's moon walk?
   four

The astronauts wore spacesuits. These suits protected them from getting too hot or too cold. Sturdy plastic helmets protected their heads. Visors protected their eyes against the sun's rays. They wore moon boots to protect their feet on the rocky surface. Gloves protected their hands. Their underwear had a built-in cooling system. They carried portable life-support systems on their backs. They needed them because there is no air on the moon. Their suits had built-in radios, so they could talk to each other and with NASA. A television camera transmitted pictures to Earth.

4. Armstrong says, "That's one small step for man, one giant leap for mankind." If he's talking about himself stepping off the ladder in the "small step" part, what is he talking about in the "giant leap" part?
   people going to the moon

5. Reread the last paragraph. Do you think the people seeing the moon landing on television could see any of Neil Armstrong's skin?
   _no_

Answer Key

Name

Week # 23

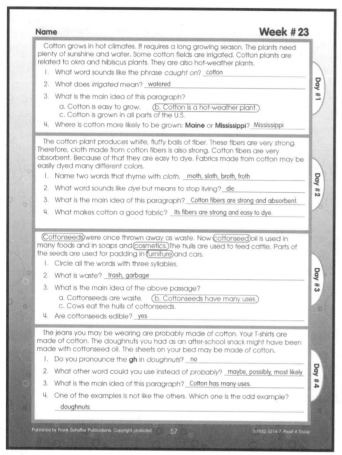

Cotton grows in hot climates. It requires a long growing season. The plants need plenty of sunshine and water. Some cotton fields are irrigated. Cotton plants are related to okra and hibiscus plants. They are also hot-weather plants.

1. What word sounds like the phrase *caught on*? __cotton__
2. What does *irrigated* mean? __watered__
3. What is the main idea of this paragraph?
   a. Cotton is easy to grow. (b. Cotton is a hot-weather plant.)
   c. Cotton is grown in all parts of the U.S.
4. Where is cotton more likely to be grown: **Maine** or **Mississippi**? __Mississippi__

Day #1

The cotton plant produces white, fluffy balls of fiber. These fibers are very strong. Therefore, cloth made from cotton fibers is also strong. Cotton fibers are very absorbent. Because of that they are easy to dye. Fabrics made from cotton may be easily dyed many different colors.

1. Name two words that rhyme with *cloth*. __moth, sloth, broth, froth__
2. What word sounds like *dye* but means to stop living? __die__
3. What is the main idea of this paragraph? __Cotton fibers are strong and absorbent.__
4. What makes cotton a good fabric? __Its fibers are strong and easy to dye.__

Day #2

(Cottonseeds) were once thrown away as waste. Now (cottonseed) oil is used in many foods and in soaps and (cosmetics.) The hulls are used to feed cattle. Parts of the seeds are used for padding in (furniture) and cars.

1. Circle all the words with three syllables.
2. What is waste? __trash, garbage__
3. What is the main idea of the above passage?
   a. Cottonseeds are waste. (b. Cottonseeds have many uses.)
   c. Cows eat the hulls of cottonseeds.
4. Are cottonseeds edible? __yes__

Day #3

The jeans you may be wearing are probably made of cotton. Your T-shirts are made of cotton. The doughnuts you had as an after-school snack might have been made with cottonseed oil. The sheets on your bed may be made of cotton.

1. Do you pronounce the **gh** in *doughnuts*? __no__
2. What other word could you use instead of *probably*? __maybe, possibly, most likely__
3. What is the main idea of this paragraph? __Cotton has many uses.__
4. One of the examples is not like the others. Which one is the odd example?
   __doughnuts__

Day #4

Name

Week # 23

Assessment

Slaves and the Crop-Over Festival

Slaves were brought to the islands in the Caribbean Sea in the 1600s. About 10 million slaves ended up in the area. The slaves were brought over to work on the sugarcane plantations. Slaves planted, cared for, and then harvested the sugarcane.

Sugarcane is a plant that has jointed stems. Sugar is found in the stems. Most sugarcane in the world is still harvested by hand.

After slaves cut the cane, they had to make it into sugar within two days or else the cane would spoil. The slaves had to work quickly. They squeezed the juice from the stems in a pressing machine. Then they boiled the juice in a big pot until it formed thick syrup. Sugar crystals formed at the bottom of the pot. Slaves put the sugar crystals in one keg. They put the juice in another. Then they took the kegs to awaiting ships. The sugar was sold in the United States and Europe. After the cane was loaded onto the ship, a slave shouted, "Crop-over!" and the celebration began. They celebrated the harvest by dancing and feasting.

This festival is still celebrated on the island of Barbados. It lasts for three weeks. There is a parade. People sell arts and crafts. Islanders make straw mats, wooden sculptures, and clay pottery. At the end of the festival, there is a band contest and fireworks.

1. Fill in the blank with a word that is spelled differently but sounds like *band*. Slaves were __banned__ from making money for themselves from the sugarcane harvest.
2. What is a plantation? __a big farm__
3. Fill in the blanks with the word *before* or *after*.
   a. Slaves boiled the juice __before__ putting it in kegs.
   b. A slave called "Crop-over" __after__ the sugarcane was loaded on the ship.
   c. Slaves squeezed the juice from sugarcane __after__ they cut the canes.
4. What is the main topic of paragraph 3? __how sugar cane is made into sugar__
5. How is the original festival different from the festival celebrated now in Barbados?
   __The one in Barbados has more events: a parade, arts and crafts sale, band contest,__ __and fireworks; the original one had dancing and eating.__

Name

Week # 24

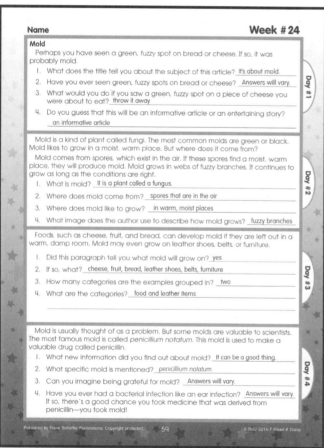

Mold

Perhaps you have seen a green, fuzzy spot on bread or cheese. If so, it was probably mold.

1. What does the title tell you about the subject of this article? __It's about mold.__
2. Have you ever seen green, fuzzy spots on bread or cheese? __Answers will vary.__
3. What would you do if you saw a green, fuzzy spot on a piece of cheese you were about to eat? __throw it away__
4. Do you guess that this will be an informative article or an entertaining story? __an informative article__

Day #1

Mold is a kind of plant called fungi. The most common molds are green or black. Mold likes to grow in a moist, warm place. But where does it come from?

Mold comes from spores, which exist in the air. If these spores find a moist, warm place, they will produce mold. Mold grows in webs of fuzzy branches. It continues to grow as long as the conditions are right.

1. What is mold? __It is a plant called a fungus.__
2. Where does mold come from? __spores that are in the air__
3. Where does mold like to grow? __in warm, moist places__
4. What image does the author use to describe how mold grows? __fuzzy branches__

Day #2

Foods, such as cheese, fruit, and bread, can develop mold if they are left out in a warm, damp room. Mold may even grow on leather shoes, belts, or furniture.

1. Did this paragraph tell you what mold will grow on? __yes__
2. If so, what? __cheese, fruit, bread, leather shoes, belts, furniture__
3. How many categories are the examples grouped in? __two__
4. What are the categories? __food and leather items__

Day #3

Mold is usually thought of as a problem. But some molds are valuable to scientists. The most famous mold is called *penicillium notatum*. This mold is used to make a valuable drug called penicillin.

1. What new information did you find out about mold? __It can be a good thing.__
2. What specific mold is mentioned? __penicillium notatum__
3. Can you imagine being grateful for mold? __Answers will vary.__
4. Have you ever had a bacterial infection like an ear infection? __Answers will vary.__ If so, there's a good chance you took medicine that was derived from penicillin—you took mold!

Day #4

Name

Week # 24

Assessment

1. Do flowers need to tell time? What else might the title mean?
   __Answers will vary.__

The Flower Clock

Have you ever seen a clock made of flowers? A Swedish man, Carl Linnaeus, made one. He was a botanist. Botanists study plants. Linnaeus lived in the eighteenth century. He grew a flower clock called "The Garden of Hours." He planted a circle of flowers. The circle represented a clock. Flowers grew at the 12:00 position. They grew at the 1:00 position. Flowers grew at each hour.

2. Name any year in the eighteenth century. __Answers will vary but must be no earlier than 1700 and no later than 1799.__

Linnaeus called the flower clock his "Watch of Flora." *Flora* means plants. His watch had 46 flowers. Each flower opened and closed at different hours. Flowers respond to light and dark. He designed the flower clock to work in Sweden. It works at latitude 60° north. It wouldn't work in the United States.

3. What is a flower clock, and how can you tell time with it?
   __a clock that is made of flowers that open or close at certain times__

Here is a list of flowers and the times they open or close in the United States. You might want to grow your own flower clock.

2:00 a.m. Moonflowers close.
5:00 a.m. Morning glories open.
9:00 a.m. Tulips open and water lilies close.
10:00 a.m. California poppies open.
12:00 noon Chicory closes.
4:00 p.m. Four o'clocks open.
5:00 p.m. Evening primroses open.
7:00 p.m. Iceland poppies close.
9:00 p.m. Moonflowers open.
10:00 p.m. Queen-of-the-Night opens.

4. List all the flowers that have a name that makes sense for the time they open.
   __morning glories, four o'clocks, evening primroses, moonflowers, Queen-of-the-Night__

5. What percentage of flowers listed are on the clock because of what time they open?
   __about 64 percent__

Answer Key

Week # 25

Lacy kicked the leaves in her yard. She didn't want to help her dad rake. She had made plans to go skating at the rink with her friends. "I just need a little help this morning, Lacy," said her dad. "You can spend the rest of the afternoon with your friends."

Lacy didn't say anything as she set to work, rhythmically moving the rake back and forth.

"Have you ever studied these leaves?" her dad asked. "It amazes me that so many of them are symmetrical."

Day #1

1. Which word has both a short **a** and long **a** in it? __amazes__
2. Is moving rhythmically moving **steadily** or **unevenly**? __steadily__
3. What season is described above? __fall__
4. What clues helped you answer #3? __Lacy and her dad are raking leaves.__

"Look at this sweet gum leaf," he said. "When you fold the leaf in half along the length of its stem, it looks the same on each side, including the veins. Something is symmetrical when there is a mirror image. The center fold line is the line of symmetry."

Day #2

1. Which word has the same **ei** sound as in *veins*: **height** or **reign**? __reign__
2. What does *symmetrical* mean? __Each side of an object is a mirror image of the other.__
3. How do you find the line of symmetry? __fold the item in half__
4. What is the line of symmetry? __The line where, if you fold an item, you'll see whether__ __the item is symmetrical.__

Jailee and her dad bent over the table drawing the plans for the tree house. (So,) what do you think, Jailee?" he asked. "Is this the size you had in mind? Are there enough windows?"

"It seems (so) small," Jailee answered.

"It's bigger than you think," her dad said. "This drawing is just a scale model."

Day #3

1. Circle the words that sound like *sew*.
2. Put a line through the sentence where *drawing* means *a picture*.
3. How does Jailee feel about the drawing? __disappointed, sad__
4. Whose idea was it to build a tree house? __Jailee's__

"A scale model is a drawing that has the same proportions, or sizes, as the true widths and lengths of a structure. The drawing reduces the actual size, but the proportions are the same. Look at the bottom of the page where you see 1 cm = 1 m."

Day #4

1. Which meaning of *scale* does the author use here?
   a. a fish scale   b. an instrument to weigh things
   (c.) something that shows the relationship between a drawing and an actual item
2. Does *reduces* mean **makes bigger** or **makes smaller**? __makes smaller__
3. What is the same in both a scale drawing and the true size of a structure? __the proportions of length and width__
4. Why is it important to have a scale on a drawing? __so you know how big the structure will be__

Week # 25

Assessment

The Kite-Eating Tree

"Another kite eaten by the tree," Manny muttered.

"My dad has a 24-foot ladder. If we knew how tall the tree was, we might be able to use it to get the kite," said Kate.

"Hey, that's a great idea!" shouted Manny. "Let's find out how tall this tree is. We did something like this in math class. We measured a stick and its shadow, and then we measured the shadow of a tree. We used equivalent fractions to calculate the height of a tree."

"That's right!" exclaimed Kate. "You go get a tape measure, and I'll find a short tree. We can measure a little tree and its shadow the same way we measured the stick."

When Manny came back, he had a tape measure, some paper, and a pencil. Kate stood beside a short pine tree. The two friends quickly set to work. They found that the height of the short tree was 4 feet tall. Its shadow was 6 feet tall. When Manny and Kate measured the shadow of the tree holding the kite, they found that its shadow was 30 feet long.

Manny quickly wrote an equation with fractions using the measurements from the trees. After Manny worked the problem, he yelled, "The tree is 20 feet tall! Your dad's ladder will reach up that high!"

1. Which words in this story start the same as *equal*?
   __equivalent, equation__
2. What is a shadow?
   __the dark shape of an object, created by the sun__
3. How do you mutter?
   __talk quietly, under your breath, without moving your mouth much__
4. What did Kate do while Manny went to get the tape measure?
   __She found a short tree.__
5. Where do you think Manny and Kate will fly the kite next time?
   __in a place away from the big tree__

Week # 26

Marie Curie

One of the greatest scientists of all time is Marie Curie.

Day #1

1. What does the title tell you about the subject of this article? __a woman named Marie Curie__
2. What new information does this sentence give you? __She is a great scientist.__
3. Is this sentence a fact or the opinion of the author? __opinion of the author__
4. Have you heard of Marie Curie? __Answers will vary.__

Marie Curie was born in Poland in 1867. She studied at a university in Paris and lived in France for most of her adult life. Along with her husband, Pierre Curie, she studied radioactivity. She was awarded the Nobel Prize in chemistry in 1911 for her work discovering radium and polonium.

Day #2

1. What details do you learn about her personal life in this paragraph? __she was born in Poland, studied in Paris, lived in France, married Pierre Curie__
2. What details do you learn about her professional life as a scientist? __She studied radioactivity, discovered radium and polonium and won the Nobel Prize.__
3. Have you heard of the Nobel Prize before? __Answers will vary.__
4. Does it sound like a big deal to win it? __yes__

The discovery of radium was a turning point in history. Some medical advances based on the research of the Curies are the X-ray and the use of radiation to treat cancer.

Day #3

1. What benefits of Marie's work are discussed here? __X-rays; radiation__
2. Does this paragraph say that Marie invented the X-ray? __no__
3. What is a *turning point in history*: something that changes life for everyone or something that changes life for only a few people? __something that changes life for everyone__
4. Do you know anyone who is a cancer survivor? __Answers will vary.__ If so, you can thank Marie Curie, in part, for that person's survival.

The Curies were both generous people. Even though they were poor for most of their lives, they did not patent any of their discoveries so that everyone could benefit from their research. Marie Curie died in 1934. The world should not forget her.

Day #4

1. Is the last sentence a fact or the author's opinion? __author's opinion__
2. Find a sentence in any part of the article that is a fact. __Answers will vary.__
3. If you were a scientist, do you think you would patent your research? Why or why not? __Answers will vary.__
4. Do you agree that Marie Curie probably is one of the greatest scientists of all time? Why or why not? __Answers will vary.__

Week # 26

1. Have you ever heard of Philo Farnsworth?
   __Answers will vary, probably, no.__

Assessment

Philo Farnsworth and Television

What would you say if someone asked who had invented the transmission, or sending, of television images? If you do not know the answer, you are not alone. Most people do not know that this was an idea of Philo Farnsworth. This is probably because a large company took Farnsworth's idea.

2. Why have most people not heard of Philo Farnsworth?
   __A large company took Farnsworth's idea.__

Farnsworth was born in a log cabin in 1906. When he was twelve, his family moved to a ranch. This put Farnsworth miles away from his school, and he rode his horse to get there.

Farnsworth was very interested in the electron and electricity. He asked one of his teachers to teach him outside of class and to let him sit in on a course for older students. The teacher agreed. He had the idea for sending television pictures when he was only fourteen.

3. What year did Farnsworth have the idea? __1920__

An article told of his invention when he was only twenty-two. How did it work? Moving images, or pictures, were broken into pinpoints of light. These pinpoints were changed into electrical impulses, or movements. Then the impulses were collected by the television set and changed back to light. People could see the images. A major magazine listed Farnsworth as one of the 100 great scientists and thinkers of the twentieth century.

4. What year did the article appear? __1928__
5. Which scientist do you think is greater: Marie Curie or Philo Farnsworth? Why?
   __Answers will vary.__

Answer Key

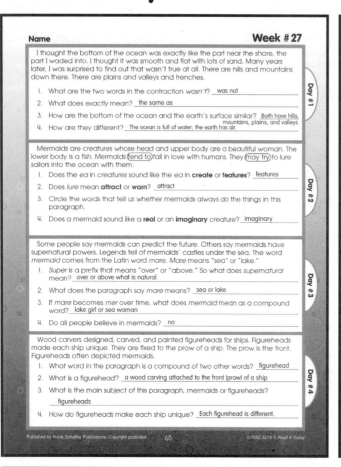

I thought the bottom of the ocean was exactly like the part near the shore, the part I waded into. I thought it was smooth and flat with lots of sand. Many years later, I was surprised to find out that wasn't true at all. There are hills and mountains down there. There are plains and valleys and trenches.

1. What are the two words in the contraction *wasn't*? __was not__
2. What does *exactly* mean? __the same as__
3. How are the bottom of the ocean and the earth's surface similar? __Both have hills, mountains, plains, and valleys.__
4. How are they different? __The ocean is full of water; the earth has air.__

Day #1

Mermaids are creatures whose head and upper body are a beautiful woman. The lower body is a fish. Mermaids (tend to) fall in love with humans. They (may try) to lure sailors into the ocean with them.

1. Does the *ea* in *creatures* sound like the *ea* in **create** or **features**? __features__
2. Does *lure* mean **attract** or **warn**? __attract__
3. Circle the words that tell us whether mermaids always do the things in this paragraph.
4. Does a mermaid sound like a **real** or an **imaginary** creature? __imaginary__

Day #2

Some people say mermaids can predict the future. Others say mermaids have supernatural powers. Legends tell of mermaids' castles under the sea. The word *mermaid* comes from the Latin word *mare*. *Mare* means "sea" or "lake."

1. *Super* is a prefix that means "over" or "above." So what does *supernatural* mean? __over or above what is natural__
2. What does the paragraph say *mare* means? __sea or lake__
3. If *mare* becomes *mer* over time, what does *mermaid* mean as a compound word? __lake girl or sea woman__
4. Do all people believe in mermaids? __no__

Day #3

Wood carvers designed, carved, and painted figureheads for ships. Figureheads made each ship unique. They are fixed to the prow of a ship. The prow is the front. Figureheads often depicted mermaids.

1. What word in the paragraph is a compound of two other words? __figurehead__
2. What is a figurehead? __a wood carving attached to the front (prow) of a ship__
3. What is the main subject of this paragraph, mermaids or figureheads? __figureheads__
4. How do figureheads make each ship unique? __Each figurehead is different.__

Day #4

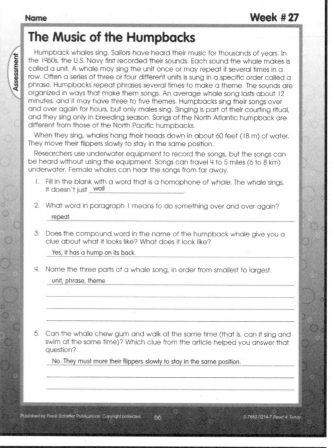

Assessment

The Music of the Humpbacks

Humpback whales sing. Sailors have heard their music for thousands of years. In the 1950s, the U.S. Navy first recorded their sounds. Each sound the whale makes is called a unit. A whale may sing the unit once or may repeat it several times in a row. Often a series of three or four different units is sung in a specific order called a phrase. Humpbacks repeat phrases several times to make a theme. The sounds are organized in ways that make them songs. An average whale song lasts about 12 minutes, and it may have three to five themes. Humpbacks sing their songs over and over again for hours, but only males sing. Singing is part of their courting ritual, and they sing only in breeding season. Songs of the North Atlantic humpback are different from those of the North Pacific humpbacks.

When they sing, whales hang their heads down in about 60 feet (18 m) of water. They move their flippers slowly to stay in the same position.

Researchers use underwater equipment to record the songs, but the songs can be heard without using the equipment. Songs can travel 4 to 5 miles (6 to 8 km) underwater. Female whales can hear the songs from far away.

1. Fill in the blank with a word that is a homophone of *whale*. The whale sings, it doesn't just __wail__.
2. What word in paragraph 1 means to do something over and over again? __repeat__
3. Does the compound word in the name of the humpback whale give you a clue about what it looks like? What does it look like? __Yes, it has a hump on its back.__
4. Name the three parts of a whale song, in order from smallest to largest. __unit, phrase, theme__
5. Can the whale chew gum and walk at the same time (that is, can it sing and swim at the same time)? Which clue from the article helped you answer that question? __No. They must move their flippers slowly to stay in the same position.__

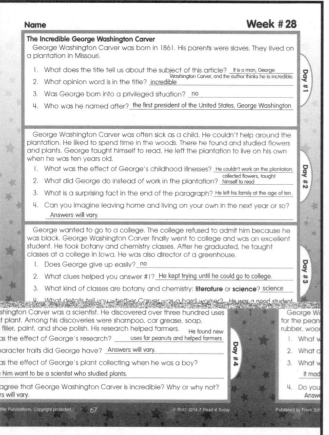

The Incredible George Washington Carver

George Washington Carver was born in 1861. His parents were slaves. They lived on a plantation in Missouri.

1. What does the title tell us about the subject of this article? __It is a man, George Washington Carver, and the author thinks he is incredible.__
2. What opinion word is in the title? __incredible__
3. Was George born into a privileged situation? __no__
4. Who was he named after? __the first president of the United States, George Washington__

Day #1

George Washington Carver was often sick as a child. He couldn't help around the plantation. He liked to spend time in the woods. There he found and studied flowers and plants. George taught himself to read. He left the plantation to live on his own when he was ten years old.

1. What was the effect of George's childhood illnesses? __He couldn't work on the plantation.__
2. What did George do instead of work in the plantation? __collected flowers, taught himself to read__
3. What is a surprising fact in the end of the paragraph? __He left his family at the age of ten.__
4. Can you imagine leaving home and living on your own in the next year or so? __Answers will vary.__

Day #2

George wanted to go to a college. The college refused to admit him because he was black. George Washington Carver finally went to college and was an excellent student. He took botany and chemistry classes. After he graduated, he taught classes at a college in Iowa. He was also director of a greenhouse.

1. Does George give up easily? __no__
2. What clues helped you answer #1? __He kept trying until he could go to college.__
3. What kind of classes are botany and chemistry: **literature** or **science**? __science__
4. What details tell you whether Carver was a hard worker? __He was a good student.__

Day #3

...shington Carver was a scientist. He discovered over three hundred uses ...t plant. Among his discoveries were shampoo, car grease, soap, ...filler, paint, and shoe polish. His research helped farmers. __He found new uses for peanuts and helped farmers.__

...as the effect of George's research?
...character traits did George have? __Answers will vary.__
...as the effect of his plant collecting when he was a boy? __It made him want to be a scientist who studied plants.__
...agree that George Washington Carver is incredible? Why or why not? ...rs will vary.

Day #4

Assessment

1. Do you think the name in the title is of a man whose first name is Duke? Or do you think it is about a man who is an English nobleman? __Answers will vary.__

Duke Ellington

When people hear Duke Ellington's name, they often think of "jazz." When he was a child, he took piano lessons. But he wasn't excited about playing the piano. Instead, he wanted to be on the baseball field.

2. What is the conflict in the above paragraph? __Duke had to take piano lessons, but he'd rather be playing baseball.__

As Ellington grew older, he heard more and more piano players. He heard music in many styles. By the time he was in high school, he had developed a true love for the piano and had written his first piece of music. He began to play the piano at parties. He also played at clubs and dances. Ellington eventually had his own musical group.

3. How was the conflict resolved? __Duke grew to love the piano.__

Ellington decided to move to New York. He played in the famous Cotton Club. Soon, his music was broadcast over the radio. He was on the road to stardom. He quickly became one of the biggest names in jazz.

4. Did Ellington listen only to jazz? __no__
5. Which of the following is **not** a lesson you can take away from this story?
   a. Don't quit an activity right away.
   b. You can make a living doing what you love.
   c. The piano is better than baseball.

Answer Key

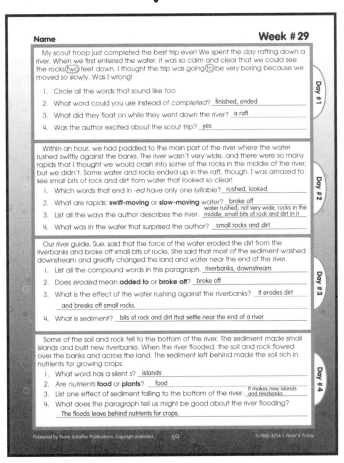

My scout troop just completed the best trip ever! We spent the day rafting down a river. When we first entered the water, it was so calm and clear that we could see the rocks (two) feet down. I thought the trip was going (to) be very boring because we moved so slowly. Was I wrong!

Day #1

1. Circle all the words that sound like *too*.
2. What word could you use instead of *completed*? _finished, ended_
3. What did they float on while they went down the river? _a raft_
4. Was the author excited about the scout trip? _yes_

Within an hour, we had paddled to the main part of the river where the water rushed swiftly against the banks. The river wasn't very wide, and there were so many rapids that I thought we would crash into some of the rocks in the middle of the river, but we didn't. Some water and rocks ended up in the raft, though. I was amazed to see small bits of rock and dirt from water that looked so clear!

Day #2

1. Which words that end in *-ed* have only one syllable? _rushed, looked_
2. What are rapids: **swift-moving** or slow-moving water? _broke off_
3. List all the ways the author describes the river. _water rushed, not very wide, rocks in the middle, small bits of rock and dirt in it_
4. What was in the water that surprised the author? _small rocks and dirt_

Our river guide, Sue, said that the force of the water eroded the dirt from the riverbanks and broke off small bits of rocks. She said that most of the sediment washed downstream and greatly changed the land and water near the end of the river.

Day #3

1. List all the compound words in this paragraph. _riverbanks, downstream_
2. Does *eroded* mean **added to** or **broke off**? _broke off_
3. What is the effect of the water rushing against the riverbanks? _It erodes dirt and breaks off small rocks._
4. What is sediment? _bits of rock and dirt that settle near the end of a river_

Some of the soil and rock fell to the bottom of the river. The sediment made small islands and built new riverbanks. When the river flooded, the soil and rock flowed over the banks and across the land. The sediment left behind made the soil rich in nutrients for growing crops.

Day #4

1. What word has a silent *s*? _islands_
2. Are *nutrients* **food** or **plants**? _food_
3. List one effect of sediment falling to the bottom of the river. _It makes new islands and riverbanks._
4. What does the paragraph tell us might be good about the river flooding? _The floods leave behind nutrients for crops._

Assessment

The Ice Hotel

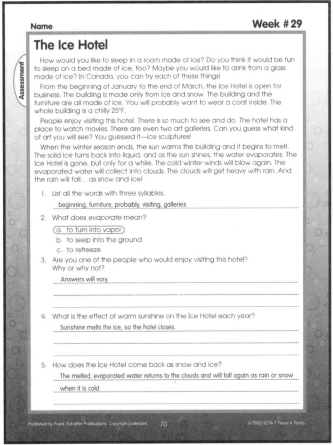

How would you like to sleep in a room made of ice? Do you think it would be fun to sleep on a bed made of ice, too? Maybe you would like to drink from a glass made of ice? In Canada, you can try each of these things!

From the beginning of January to the end of March, the Ice Hotel is open for business. The building is made only from ice and snow. The building and the furniture are all made of ice. You will probably want to wear a coat inside. The whole building is a chilly 25°F.

People enjoy visiting this hotel. There is so much to see and do. The hotel has a place to watch movies. There are even two art galleries. Can you guess what kind of art you will see? You guessed it—ice sculptures!

When the winter season ends, the sun warms the building and it begins to melt. The solid ice turns back into liquid, and as the sun shines, the water evaporates. The Ice Hotel is gone, but only for a while. The cold winter winds will blow again. The evaporated water will collect into clouds. The clouds will get heavy with rain. And the rain will fall… as snow and ice!

1. List all the words with three syllables.
   beginning, furniture, probably, visiting, galleries

2. What does *evaporate* mean?
   (a. to turn into vapor)
   b. to seep into the ground
   c. to refreeze

3. Are you one of the people who would enjoy visiting this hotel? Why or why not?
   Answers will vary.

4. What is the effect of warm sunshine on the Ice Hotel each year?
   Sunshine melts the ice, so the hotel closes.

5. How does the Ice Hotel come back as snow and ice?
   The melted, evaporated water returns to the clouds and will fall again as rain or snow when it is cold.

Letter to Grandma

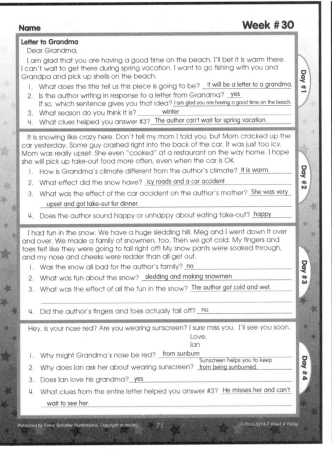

Dear Grandma,

I am glad that you are having a good time on the beach. I'll bet it is warm there. I can't wait to get there during spring vacation. I want to go fishing with you and Grandpa and pick up shells on the beach.

Day #1

1. What does the title tell us this piece is going to be? _It will be a letter to a grandma._
2. Is the author writing in response to a letter from Grandma? _yes_
   If so, which sentence gives you that idea? _I am glad you are having a good time on the beach._
3. What season do you think it is? _winter_
4. What clues helped you answer #3? _The author can't wait for spring vacation._

It is snowing like crazy here. Don't tell my mom I told you, but Mom cracked up the car yesterday. Some guy crashed right into the back of the car. It was just too icy. Mom was really upset. She even "cooked" at a restaurant on the way home. I hope she will pick up take-out food more often, even when the car is OK.

Day #2

1. How is Grandma's climate different from the author's climate? _It is warm._
2. What effect did the snow have? _icy roads and a car accident_
3. What was the effect of the car accident on the author's mother? _She was very upset and got take-out for dinner._
4. Does the author sound happy or unhappy about eating take-out? _happy_

I had fun in the snow. We have a huge sledding hill. Meg and I went down it over and over. We made a family of snowmen, too. Then we got cold. My fingers and toes felt like they were going to fall right off! My snow pants were soaked through, and my nose and cheeks were redder than all get out.

Day #3

1. Was the snow all bad for the author's family? _no_
2. What was fun about the snow? _sledding and making snowmen_
3. What was the effect of all the fun in the snow? _The author got cold and wet._
4. Did the author's fingers and toes actually fall off? _no_

Hey, is your nose red? Are you wearing sunscreen? I sure miss you. I'll see you soon.
Love,
Ian

Day #4

1. Why might Grandma's nose be red? _from sunburn_
2. Why does Ian ask her about wearing sunscreen? _Sunscreen helps you to keep from being sunburned._
3. Does Ian love his grandma? _yes_
4. What clues from the entire letter helped you answer #3? _He misses her and can't wait to see her._

---

1. What is the greatest gift you've ever been given?
   Answers will vary.

Assessment

The Greatest Gift

When Rena walked in the door at home, her little brother grabbed her by the arm. "Rena, Rena, will you make a picture for Grandpa's birthday? I wrote a poem for him, but I want to put it with a great big picture. And I want you to do it because you're such a great artist."

Rena smiled. "Okay, Oscar. Grab all those old pictures from the box."

2. What did the first two paragraphs tell us about the three characters in this story?
   Oscar writes poems; Rena is an artist; Grandpa is having a birthday

Oscar skipped out of the room. A few minutes later, he dashed in, carrying Grandpa's photos. It was hard to piece them together because they were all torn, and they were faded, too.

At the art studio, Rena laid the torn and faded photos across a table so she could arrange them in a special way. For weeks, Rena worked with her paints on a big canvas. She placed every stroke and chose every color with great care.

3. What kind of art does Rena do?
   She paints.

On Grandpa's birthday, Oscar read his poem. Then Rena gave Grandpa the painting. Tears filled Grandpa's eyes. "The poem was wonderful, and the painting… the painting shows my old friends and my old neighborhood in a way that makes me feel as though I'm there all over again. Rena, you've shown me how special all these people have been in my life. You and Oscar are wonderful."

4. What is the time frame of the story?
   Answers will vary.

5. Why did Grandpa cry after he saw the painting?
   Answers will vary.

Answer Key

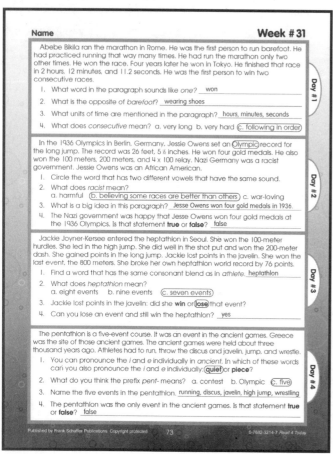

Week # 31

Abebe Bikila ran the marathon in Rome. He was the first person to run barefoot. He had practiced running that way many times. He had run the marathon only two other times. He won the race. Four years later he won in Tokyo. He finished that race in 2 hours, 12 minutes, and 11.2 seconds. He was the first person to win two consecutive races.

1. What word in the paragraph sounds like *one*? __won__
2. What is the opposite of *barefoot*? __wearing shoes__
3. What units of time are mentioned in the paragraph? __hours, minutes, seconds__
4. What does *consecutive* mean? a. very long b. very hard (c. following in order)

Day #1

In the 1936 Olympics in Berlin, Germany, Jessie Owens set an (Olympic) record for the long jump. The record was 26 feet, 5½ inches. He won four gold medals. He also won the 100 meters, 200 meters, and 4 x 100 relay. Nazi Germany was a racist government. Jessie Owens was an African American.

1. Circle the word that has two different vowels that have the same sound.
2. What does *racist* mean?
   a. harmful (b. believing some races are better than others) c. war-loving
3. What is a big idea in this paragraph? __Jesse Owens won four gold medals in 1936.__
4. The Nazi government was happy that Jesse Owens won four gold medals at the 1936 Olympics. Is that statement **true** or **false**? __false__

Day #2

Jackie Joyner-Kersee entered the heptathlon in Seoul. She won the 100-meter hurdles. She led in the high jump. She did well in the shot put and won the 200-meter dash. She gained points in the long jump. Jackie lost points in the javelin. She won the last event, the 800 meters. She broke her own heptathlon world record by 76 points.

1. Find a word that has the same consonant blend as in *athlete*. __heptathlon__
2. What does *heptathlon* mean?
   a. eight events b. nine events (c. seven events)
3. Jackie lost points in the javelin: did she **win** or (lose) that event?
4. Can you lose an event and still win the heptathlon? __yes__

Day #3

The pentathlon is a five-event course. It was an event in the ancient games. Greece was the site of those ancient games. The ancient games were held about three thousand years ago. Athletes had to run, throw the discus and javelin, jump, and wrestle.

1. You can pronounce the *i* and *e* individually in *ancient*. In which of these words can you also pronounce the *i* and *e* individually: (quiet) or **piece**?
2. What do you think the prefix *pent-* means? a. contest b. Olympic (c. five)
3. Name the five events in the pentathlon. __running, discus, javelin, high jump, wrestling__
4. The pentathlon was the only event in the ancient games. Is that statement **true** or **false**? __false__

Day #4

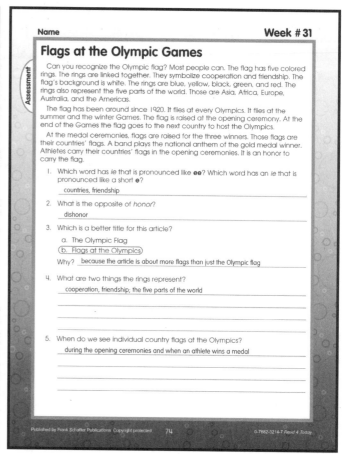

Week # 31

Assessment

Flags at the Olympic Games

Can you recognize the Olympic flag? Most people can. The flag has five colored rings. The rings are linked together. They symbolize cooperation and friendship. The flag's background is white. The rings are blue, yellow, black, green, and red. The rings also represent the five parts of the world. Those are Asia, Africa, Europe, Australia, and the Americas.

The flag has been around since 1920. It flies at every Olympics. It flies at the summer and the winter Games. The flag is raised at the opening ceremony. At the end of the Games the flag goes to the next country to host the Olympics.

At the medal ceremonies, flags are raised for the three winners. Those flags are their countries' flags. A band plays the national anthem of the gold medal winner. Athletes carry their countries' flags in the opening ceremonies. It is an honor to carry the flag.

1. Which word has *ie* that is pronounced like *ee*? Which word has an *ie* that is pronounced like a short *e*?
   __countries, friendship__

2. What is the opposite of *honor*?
   __dishonor__

3. Which is a better title for this article?
   a. The Olympic Flag
   (b. Flags at the Olympics)
   Why? __because the article is about more flags than just the Olympic flag__

4. What are two things the rings represent?
   __cooperation, friendship; the five parts of the world__

5. When do we see individual country flags at the Olympics?
   __during the opening ceremonies and when an athlete wins a medal__

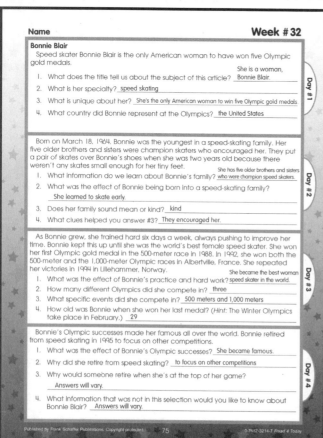

Week # 32

Bonnie Blair

Speed skater Bonnie Blair is the only American woman to have won five Olympic gold medals.

1. What does the title tell us about the subject of this article? __She is a woman, Bonnie Blair.__
2. What is her specialty? __speed skating__
3. What is unique about her? __She's the only American woman to win five Olympic gold medals.__
4. What country did Bonnie represent at the Olympics? __the United States__

Day #1

Born on March 18, 1964, Bonnie was the youngest in a speed-skating family. Her five older brothers and sisters were champion skaters who encouraged her. They put a pair of skates over Bonnie's shoes when she was two years old because there weren't any skates small enough for her tiny feet.

1. What information do we learn about Bonnie's family? __who were champion speed skaters__ (She has five older brothers and sisters)
2. What was the effect of Bonnie being born into a speed-skating family? __She learned to skate early.__
3. Does her family sound mean or kind? __kind__
4. What clues helped you answer #3? __They encouraged her.__

Day #2

As Bonnie grew, she trained hard six days a week, always pushing to improve her time. Bonnie kept this up until she was the world's best female speed skater. She won her first Olympic gold medal in the 500-meter race in 1988. In 1992, she won both the 500-meter and the 1,000-meter Olympic races in Albertville, France. She repeated her victories in 1994 in Lillehammer, Norway.

1. What was the effect of Bonnie's practice and hard work? __speed skater in the world__ (She became the best woman)
2. How many different Olympics did she compete in? __three__
3. What specific events did she compete in? __500 meters and 1,000 meters__
4. How old was Bonnie when she won her last medal? (*Hint:* The Winter Olympics take place in February.) __29__

Day #3

Bonnie's Olympic successes made her famous all over the world. Bonnie retired from speed skating in 1995 to focus on other competitions.

1. What was the effect of Bonnie's Olympic successes? __She became famous.__
2. Why did she retire from speed skating? __to focus on other competitions__
3. Why would someone retire when she's at the top of her game? __Answers will vary.__
4. What information that was not in this selection would you like to know about Bonnie Blair? __Answers will vary.__

Day #4

Week # 32

Assessment

1. Do not read the paragraphs. Just looking at the title, do you think it sets up an article about the use of animals at the Olympics or about animals competing at the Olympics?
   __Answers will vary.__

Animals at the Olympics

The Olympics are games that show the strength and speed of human athletes. The fastest, strongest person wins. But have you ever wondered what might happen if animals were allowed at the Olympics? Do you still think humans would win?

2. Do not read the next two paragraphs. Do you think humans would win against animals?
   __Answers will vary.__

The fastest human was clocked at a speed of nearly 27 miles per hour (mph). Many animals can beat that time. A housecat can run 30 mph. The antelope is even faster. It runs at speeds over 60 mph. But the Olympic winner would be the cheetah. This cat runs over 70 mph.

3. Which animals would win the gold, silver, and bronze medals in the running race?
   __cheetah–gold; antelope–silver; house cat–bronze__

There are two main jumping events in the Olympics. One is height, and the other is distance. The record for the longest human jump is 29 feet. The highest jump without a pole is about 8 feet. The puma would beat humans in both events. It can jump 12 feet high and cover a distance of 39 feet in one jump. However, the animal winning the long jump would the kangaroo. It can jump an amazing 42 feet!

4. What is the difference in feet between a kangaroo's jump and the longest human jump?
   __13 feet__

5. How does the author feel about the kangaroo's ability to jump?
   __The author is impressed.__

Answer Key

Sri Lanka is a small island located in the Indian Ocean, near southeast India. The island celebrates a holiday called Poya. Poya has been around since about 250 B.C. Poya honors the full moon. Everything on the island closes for Poya: stores, schools, offices, and movies. The problem is that Poya comes once a month. Why? There's a full moon once a month. Business leaders complain that the holiday disrupts their economy.

Day #1

1. What word starts with a hard **c** sound? __complain__
2. What does the word *disrupts* mean?
   a. improves or helps   b. leaves out   (c. interrupts or disturbs)
3. How many Poya celebrations are there each year? __12__
4. Who likes Poya more: **school kids** or **business leaders**? __school kids__

The Jewish Sukkoth is an eight-day harvest festival held in September or October. It celebrates the harvest of grapes and olives, two important crops in the Middle East. It is also a time for giving thanks for food and for friendship. Jewish people around the world celebrate Sukkoth. People built wooden booths called Sukkoth. The word also means "shelter."

Day #2

1. List all the words that start with an **s/soft c** sound. __Sukkoth, September, celebrate__
2. What does *Sukkoth* mean? __shelter__
3. What is the main idea of this paragraph: **Jewish people build wooden booths** or (**Jewish people celebrate a harvest festival they call Sukkoth**)?
4. What is the American holiday that is a time for giving thanks for food and for friendship? __Thanksgiving__

Many islands have unique styles of music. Some are calypso, ska, reggae, and salsa. Salsa came from Cuba. Calypso is the music of the islands of Trinidad and Tobago. Calypso was influenced by jazz. Ska is from Jamaica. So is reggae. Reggae is a mixture of calypso and rap music.

Day #3

1. What word ends with the same sound that begins *aeroplane*? __reggae__
2. What does *unique* mean?
   a. strange   (b. the only one of its kind)   c. popular
3. What is the main subject in this paragraph: (**the music**) or **the islands**?
4. Which island has two styles of music attributed to it? __Jamaica__

Islands have unique musical instruments. The steel drum originated on Trinidad in the 1930s. Steel drums are called pans. They are made of recycled oil drums. Island music has an African beat. Drums probably came to the islands with African slaves.

Island musicians also use a rhumba box. The rhumba box is like the African thumb piano. It is a wooden box with a hole in the middle. On top are metal keys. Musicians pluck the keys.

Day #4

1. What word that has to do with poetry starts with *rh* like *rhumba*? __rhyme__
2. How do you pluck a musical instrument? __pull and let go of a string with your finger__
3. What is the rhumba box compared with? __African thumb piano__
4. What materials are rhumba boxes made of? __wood and metal__

Assessment

Pongol

Pongol is a festival in India. It is a rice festival. Rice is an important crop in India. Indians celebrate Pongol in January. This festival falls after the end of the monsoon season, the wet season in India.

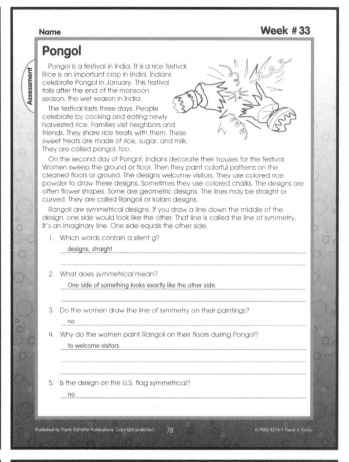

The festival lasts three days. People celebrate by cooking and eating newly harvested rice. Families visit neighbors and friends. They share rice treats with them. These sweet treats are made of rice, sugar, and milk. They are called pongol, too.

On the second day of Pongol, Indians decorate their houses for the festival. Women sweep the ground or floor. Then they paint colorful patterns on the cleaned floors or ground. The designs welcome visitors. They use colored rice powder to draw these designs. Sometimes they use colored chalks. The designs are often flower shapes. Some are geometric designs. The lines may be straight or curved. They are called Rangoli or kolam designs.

Rangoli are symmetrical designs. If you draw a line down the middle of the design, one side would look like the other. That line is called the line of symmetry. It's an imaginary line. One side equals the other side.

1. Which words contain a silent *g*?
   __designs, straight__

2. What does *symmetrical* mean?
   __One side of something looks exactly like the other side.__

3. Do the women draw the line of symmetry on their paintings?
   __no__

4. Why do the women paint Rangoli on their floors during Pongol?
   __to welcome visitors__

5. Is the design on the U.S. flag symmetrical?
   __no__

The Crow and the Fox

A crow found a piece of cheese on the ground. It quickly swooped down to pick up the food and perched on a limb to enjoy the tasty treat. A fox wandered by and saw this.

Day #1

1. This is one of Aesop's fables. What is a fable?
   a. a funny story   b. a true story   (c. a story that teaches a lesson)
2. What does the title tell us about the characters in this fable? __They are a fox and a crow__
3. Do we meet both characters in the first paragraph? __yes__
4. What was the first thing the crow did after grabbing the cheese? __flew to a tree branch__

"Good afternoon, Crow," the fox called out politely. "How lovely you look today! I bet your voice is just as beautiful so that you sing the sweetest melodies of all the birds in the forest."

Day #2

1. Why was the fox saying nice things to the crow?
   a. he wanted to eat the crow   (b. he wanted the cheese)
   c. he wanted to hear the crow sing
2. Have you ever heard a crow before? If so, do you think it is a beautiful sound? __Answers will vary.__
3. What about the crow did the fox actually compliment? __her looks__
4. What time of day does this fable take place in? __the afternoon__

The crow believed every word that the fox spoke about her beauty. The crow lifted her beak into the air and opened her mouth to show the fox her musical voice. Just as she did this, the cheese fell out of her mouth. The fox grabbed the cheese and hungrily devoured it.

Day #3

1. Why did the crow drop the cheese?
   (a. she opened her mouth to sing)   b. she wanted to share
   c. she wanted to yell at the fox
2. Do you think the fox meant those compliments? __Answers will vary.__
3. What was the first thing the fox did after grabbing the cheese? __ate it__
4. What clues tell you that the fox was probably hungrier than the crow? __The fox ate the cheese right away.__

The fox smiled slyly as he walked away, very pleased with his clever trick. As he strolled back into the woods, he called back to the speechless crow, "I will give you some words of wisdom, little Crow. Do not trust those who praise you with so many compliments."

Day #4

1. Restate the fox's message in your own words. __Answers will vary.__
2. What other message works?
   a. Always share your cheese.   b. Always compliment others.
   (c. Never listen to a fox.)
3. Has anyone ever complimented you to get you to do something he or she wanted? If so, did it work? __Answers will vary.__
4. Have you ever complimented someone to get what you wanted from him or her? If so, did it work? __Answers will vary.__

---

1. Do you think this one of Aesop's fables? Why or why not?
   __yes; answers will vary__

Assessment

The Oak and the Reeds

A mighty oak grew along a riverbank. Its trunk was thick, and its branches reached upward into the sky. It towered proudly above a patch of reeds that grew below it along the edge of the water.

2. What kind of thing are the two characters in this fable?
   __plants__

On most days, a breeze blew across the river. The leaves of the mighty oak danced, but its branches held firmly in place. The oak laughed at the reeds because the wind was not so kind to them. The reeds trembled and shook as they struggled to stand up straight. But the reeds did not mind the laughter of the oak; after all, the tree was so much bigger and stronger.

Then one day, a terrible hurricane approached the river. Its violent winds pulled up the roots of the mighty oak and tossed it to the ground. When the storm was over, the great tree lay in the patch of reeds.

3. How is the oak tree different from the reeds?
   __The oak tree is bigger and doesn't bend easily; the reeds are smaller and bend easily.__

The oak spoke sadly, "The strong winds were able to pick me up and throw me to the ground like a stick. Yet you reeds were able to stay rooted even though you are much smaller. How could this be?"

One reed spoke. "We may be small, but we know how to bend, whether the wind blows gently or violently. You, mighty oak, were too proud and did not know how to bend."

4. What was the cause of the oak tree falling?
   __the violent winds of the hurricane__

5. What is the lesson of this fable?
   (a. It can be better to be flexible than to be strong.)
   b. It's okay to laugh at those smaller than you.
   c. Stay out of the way of a hurricane.

Answer Key

Green plants are like factories. Plant factories make two kinds of food: one is sugar, and the other is starch. Almost all fruits and (vegetables) you eat contain some form of sugar or starch. Fruits like apples, (oranges), cherries, pears, and even lemons contain sugar; vegetables like potatoes, corn, and beans contain starch.

1. Circle words with a soft **g** sound and put a line through words with a hard **g** sound.
2. What is a factory? _a place where things are made_
3. With what does the author compare green plants? _a factory_
4. What two kinds of food do plant factories make? _sugar and starch_

Day #1

Green plants are made up of cells just like you are. A cell is the smallest structural unit of a living organism, whether it is a plant or an animal. Because they are so small, cells can be seen only through a microscope. Inside the cells are chloroplasts, which contain chlorophyll and carotene. They manufacture the sugar and starch; therefore, they are the machines of the plant factory.

1. List the words that start with the same starting sound as *clean*. _chloroplast chlorophyll_
2. With what is a microscope? _an instrument you use to look at small things_
3. What is compared with the machines of a factory? _the cells of a living organism_
4. Can you see cells with the naked eye? _no_

Day #2

There are two kinds of doors in plant factories. One kind is called stomata. Stomata are tiny holes in the leaves that allow air to move in and out through these doors. Plants use carbon dioxide and then release oxygen (back) into the air. Roots are the second kind of (door) Water travels into root hairs of the plant. This movement is called capillary action.

1. Circle words with *oo* that have the same vowel sound as **boots**. Put a line through words with *oo* containing the same vowel sound as **floor**.
2. What are stomata? _tiny holes in plant leaves_
3. Which is a better title for this paragraph: **Stomata in the Leaves** or **Doors of the Factory**? _Doors of the Factory_
4. What are the two kinds of doors in plant factories? _stomata and roots_

Day #3

Plants use storerooms to store their food. Carrot plants store their food in roots, while maple trees store their food in trunks. Lettuce plants store their food in leaves, peas store their food in seeds, and peach trees store their food in the fruit.

1. Find a compound word in this paragraph. _storerooms_
2. What word could you use instead of *store* as it is used above? _keep, save_
3. What is the topic sentence of this paragraph? _Plants use storerooms to store their fruit._
4. Name three plants and their storerooms. _carrot, root; lettuce, leaves; peas, seeds; peach tree, fruit; maple tree, trunk_

Day #4

Assessment

The Brain

Have you ever watched a coach during a ball game? The coach tells players where to go and what to do as things are happening in the game. Your brain is like your coach. Information from your five senses—touch, smell, hearing, taste, sight—races to your brain. Your brain sorts out the information and lets your body know what to do.

Your brain has three main parts, the medulla, cerebrum, and cerebellum. Perhaps you have heard someone talk about "gray matter" while discussing intelligence. This refers to the cerebrum. The cerebrum is large, and its outside layer is gray and looks wrinkled. The cerebrum, the cerebral cortex, springs to work when you are doing something that requires a good deal of thought. If you are taking a test, talking to a friend, or reading directions to put together a new bicycle, your cerebrum is busy.

As you try to keep your balance on your bicycle, it is your cerebellum that is called to work. The cerebellum is in control of balance and coordination. It is much smaller than the cerebrum.

The medulla is your brain stem. It is the lowest part of your brain. The medulla controls breathing and heart rate.

The next time you put together a bicycle, and then hop on and gasp for breath after riding up a hill, you will know that all the parts of your brain have been very busy.

1. List the words that have to do with the brain that start with a soft **c** sound. _cerebrum, cerebellum, cerebral_
2. What is the cerebral cortex? _the cerebrum_
3. To what does the idiom *gray matter* refer? _our brain_
4. What does this article compare your brain with? Why? _a coach, because the coach tells his players what to do and our brain tells our body what to do_
5. Make a chart that details which part of the brain controls which function and one example of that function.

   Example:
   cerebrum-things that require thought-taking a test

Aboriginal Art

The Aboriginal people in Australia were hunters and gatherers. They were also skilled artists. They have been painting and carving rocks for thousands of years. The paintings are found mostly in caves throughout central Australia. The oldest paintings that have been discovered are about 30,000 years old.

1. What does the title tell us about the subject of this article? _It will be about Aboriginal art._
2. Where do Aborigines live? _Australia_
3. What details does the paragraph tell you about them? _They were hunters and gatherers and artists who painted and carved rocks, they've been around for at least 30,000 years._
4. Aborigines are the original dwellers of Australia. What do they compare with in the United States? _Native Americans_

Day #1

Aborigine artists use natural paints made from the earth, tree bark, and plants. Red comes from ochre and hematite. Ochre and hematite are minerals. Black comes from charcoal. White comes from gypsum, a mineral found in rocks. It's used to make cement.

1. Where does the paragraph tell us Aborigine artists find their paints? _earth, tree bark, plants_
2. What is the one example of a color that does not come from a mineral? _black from charcoal_
3. Does this paragraph give you any examples of colors from plants? _no_
4. What do Aborigine paintings have in common with cement? _Both use gypsum._

Day #2

Aborigine musicians have unusual musical instruments. One is called the didgeridoo. It is made from a hollowed-out log. It is a wind instrument that is played by blowing wind through it. A didgeridoo may be painted with the same elaborate designs found in the rock paintings.

1. So far, in this article, what two things do Aborigine artists paint? _caves, didgeridoos_
2. Does the didgeridoo sound like it is a small or a large instrument? _large_
3. Did Aborigine musicians find their musical instruments like the artists found their paints—from nature? _yes_
4. What clues helped you answer #3? _The didgeridoo is made from a log, which comes from nature._

Day #3

Aborigines paint themselves for special religious ceremonies. These ceremonies are a part of their traditional culture. Their religion links them to the land and nature. They express themselves artistically through music making, dancing, singing, and storytelling.

1. List all the things the article says Aborigine artists paint on. _caves, didgeridoos, themselves_
2. What is important to their religion? _land and nature_
3. What do Aborigine people do in their religious ceremonies? _make music, sing, dance, tell stories_
4. How does painting come into their religious ceremonies? _They paint themselves and their didgeridoos._

Day #4

Assessment

1. What would you guess the topic of this article is, just based on the title? _Answers will vary but have something to do with sleep._

Dreamtime

The Aborigines have been in Australia for thousands of years. Some scientists believe they have been there for about 30,000 years. The name *Aborigine* means "the very first." They were the very first people in Australia. They believe that ancestral beings created the world in a time very long ago, called Dreamtime. Elders know the history of Dreamtime. They pass it on to younger generations.

2. What is the Dreamtime in this article? Was it what you expected from the title? _Dreamtime is when the world was created. Yes, it is different from what I expected._

Dreamtime explains the beginning of the world. Aborigines believe that during Dreamtime, spirits created the land, animals, plants, and humans. The spirit beings didn't die. They joined with nature. They live in the Aborigine beliefs and sacred rituals. Dreamtime explains the rules for living. It explains the rules for social behavior. It explains the whole structure of society.

3. List all the things the second paragraph says Aborigines believe Dreamtime explains. _the beginning of the work, rules for living, rules for social behavior, the structure of society_

Dreamtime paintings are usually symmetrical. They are made of arcs, circles, and ovals. Some lines are straight. Some lines are curved. Specific patterns and designs have names. The men paint Dreamtime symbols and patterns on their bodies for special ceremonies. The ceremonies are called corroborees.

4. Name the geometric shapes used in Dreamtime paintings. _arc, circle, oval_
5. What clues from the article tell you that Dreamtime has a central place in Aborigine life and culture? _It explains the beginning of the world and everything about Aboriginal life._

Answer Key

Week # 37 (page 85)

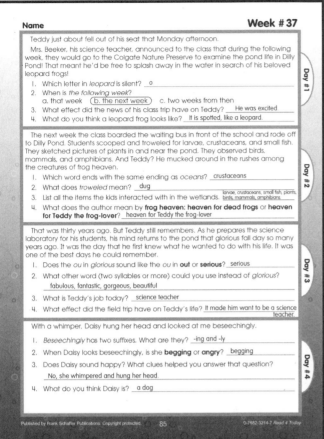

Name

Teddy just about fell out of his seat that Monday afternoon.

Mrs. Beeker, his science teacher, announced to the class that during the following week, they would go to the Colgate Nature Preserve to examine the pond life in Dilly Pond! That meant he'd be free to splash away in the water in search of his beloved leopard frogs!

Day #1
1. Which letter in *leopard* is silent? _o_
2. When is *the following week*?
   a. that week (b. the next week) c. two weeks from then
3. What effect did the news of his class trip have on Teddy? _He was excited_
4. What do you think a leopard frog looks like? _It is spotted, like a leopard_

The next week the class boarded the waiting bus in front of the school and rode off to Dilly Pond. Students scooped and troweled for larvae, crustaceans, and small fish. They sketched pictures of plants in and near the pond. They observed birds, mammals, and amphibians. And Teddy? He mucked around in the rushes among the creatures of frog heaven.

Day #2
1. Which word ends with the same ending as *oceans*? _crustaceans_
2. What does *troweled* mean? _dug_
3. List all the items the kids interacted with in the wetlands. _larvae, crustaceans, small fish, plants, birds, mammals, amphibians_
4. What does the author mean by *frog heaven: heaven for dead frogs* or *heaven for Teddy the frog-lover*? _heaven for Teddy the frog-lover_

That was thirty years ago. But Teddy still remembers. As he prepares the science laboratory for his students, his mind returns to the pond that glorious fall day so many years ago. It was the day that he first knew what he wanted to do with his life. It was one of the best days he could remember.

Day #3
1. Does the *ou* in *glorious* sound like the *ou* in **out** or **serious**? _serious_
2. What other word (two syllables or more) could you use instead of *glorious*? _fabulous, fantastic, gorgeous, beautiful_
3. What is Teddy's job today? _science teacher_
4. What effect did the field trip have on Teddy's life? _It made him want to be a science teacher._

With a whimper, Daisy hung her head and looked at me beseechingly.

Day #4
1. *Beseechingly* has two suffixes. What are they? _-ing and -ly_
2. When Daisy looks beseechingly, is she **begging** or **angry**? _begging_
3. Does Daisy sound happy? What clues helped you answer that question? _No, she whimpered and hung her head._
4. What do you think Daisy is? _a dog_

Week # 37 (page 86)

Name — *Assessment*

Aquarium Competition

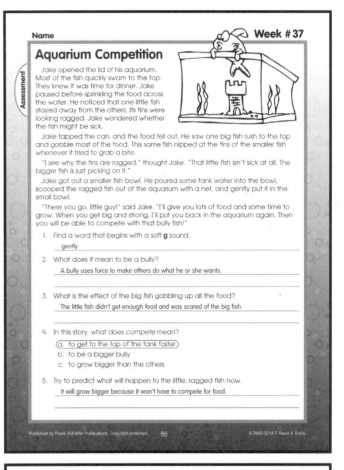

Jake opened the lid of his aquarium. Most of the fish quickly swam to the top. They knew it was time for dinner. Jake paused before sprinkling the food across the water. He noticed that one little fish stayed away from the others. Its fins were looking ragged. Jake wondered whether the fish might be sick.

Jake tapped the can, and the food fell out. He saw one big fish rush to the top and gobble most of the food. This same fish nipped at the fins of the smaller fish whenever it tried to grab a bite.

"I see why the fins are ragged," thought Jake. "That little fish isn't sick at all. The bigger fish is just picking on it."

Jake got out a smaller fish bowl. He poured some tank water into the bowl, scooped the ragged fish out of the aquarium with a net, and gently put it in the small bowl.

"There you go, little guy!" said Jake. "I'll give you lots of food and some time to grow. When you get big and strong, I'll put you back in the aquarium again. Then you will be able to compete with that bully fish!"

1. Find a word that begins with a soft **g** sound.
   gently
2. What does it mean to be a bully?
   A bully uses force to make others do what he or she wants.
3. What is the effect of the big fish gobbling up all the food?
   The little fish didn't get enough food and was scared of the big fish.
4. In this story, what does *compete* mean?
   (a. to get to the top of the tank faster)
   b. to be a bigger bully
   c. to grow bigger than the others
5. Try to predict what will happen to the little, ragged fish now.
   It will grow bigger because it won't have to compete for food.

Week # 38 (page 87)

Name

Animal Mysteries

As long as people have studied animals, they have wondered why animals act certain ways. Animal behavior can be a real mystery.

Day #1
1. What does the title tell us about the topic of this article? _It will be about mysteries that have to do with animals._
2. What kind of mystery is the topic here? _animal behavior_
3. How do people come across these mysterious behaviors? _by studying animals_
4. What is a mystery? _something that people can't explain_

One mystery has to do with some animals' strange behavior before earthquakes. Horses and cattle stampede, seabirds screech, dogs howl, and some animals even come out of hibernation early before an earthquake begins.

Day #2
1. What is the first mystery? _how animals behave before an earthquake_
2. What specific details does the author include? _stampeding, screeching, howling, coming out of hibernation_
3. Why might it be helpful to know about these behaviors if you lived in earthquake country? _You might know an earthquake is coming._
4. Is the behavior for each animal something it doesn't do normally? Or is it unusual that the animal behave this way right before an earthquake? _that they do it right before an earthquake_

Another mystery involves birds and ants. No one can explain why a bird will pick up an ant in its beak and rub the ant over its feathers again and again. This is called "anting," and birds have been known to do this for an hour without stopping.

Day #3
1. What is the mystery in this paragraph? _why birds rub ants on their feathers_
2. Does the activity have a special name? If so, what is it? _yes; anting_
3. Do any words give you the idea that the author finds this mystery funny? _no_
4. Do you find it funny? Why or why not? _Answers will vary._

One animal mystery is very sad. For hundreds of years, some whales have swum into shallow waters and mysteriously grounded themselves on a beach where they might die. Reports of beached whales occur about five times a year somewhere in the world.

Day #4
1. What is the mystery in this paragraph? _why whales swim into shallow waters_
2. Does the author give an opinion about this mystery? _yes_
3. If so, what opinion? _the whales beaching themselves is sad_
4. How do you think the author feels about animals? _interested in, fascinated by_

Week # 38 (page 88)

Name — *Assessment*

1. Without reading the poem, what do you already know about backpacks?
   I use them for carrying books; they can be heavy

My Backpack
Anonymous

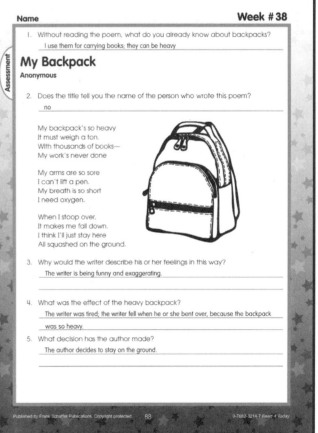

2. Does the title tell you the name of the person who wrote this poem?
   _no_

My backpack's so heavy
It must weigh a ton.
With thousands of books—
My work's never done

My arms are so sore
I can't lift a pen.
My breath is so short
I need oxygen.

When I stoop over,
It makes me fall down.
I think I'll just stay here
All squashed on the ground.

3. Why would the writer describe his or her feelings in this way?
   The writer is being funny and exaggerating.
4. What was the effect of the heavy backpack?
   The writer was tired; the writer fell when he or she bent over, because the backpack was so heavy.
5. What decision has the author made?
   The author decides to stay on the ground.

Answer Key

Name   **Week # 39**

Have you ever had the pleasure of watching a praying mantis capture its prey? It raises its forelegs, as if in prayer, and waits patiently for an unsuspecting insect. When its prey comes within striking distance, the mantis thrusts its forelegs out and grabs its insect victim. The clever praying mantis is actually a preying master.

Day #1

1. Which two words sound the same but are spelled differently?
   praying and preying
2. What does the prefix *un-* in *unsuspecting* mean? _not_
3. What words does the author use to refer to the insect? _prey, victim_
4. Why is it called a *praying* mantis? _Its front legs make it look like it's praying when it waits for prey._

A mantis relies on its keen vision for capturing prey. Its triangular face supports two huge compound eyes. The mantis may tilt its head as if to get a better look at you, but its compound eyes allow it to see in almost all directions. In the center of its two eyes, the mantis also has three other tiny eyes, called ocelli, which help the mantis distinguish dark and light.

Day #2

1. Does the *gu* in *distinguish* sound like the *gu* in **guide** or **anguish**? _anguish_
2. What word could you use instead of *keen*? _sharp, precise, good_
3. What is the main subject of this paragraph? _the mantis's eyes_
4. What does it mean that the mantis has *compound eyes*? _Its eyes are made up of a group of other eyes._

In the early morning or late afternoon, you may find a praying mantis hanging upside down with its forelegs folded. It is not resting; the mantis is waiting. It is waiting for a fly, bee, butterfly, grasshopper, or caterpillar. The mantis eats only insects. It has no need even for water since it gets plenty from the body of its prey.

Day #3

1. Name at least three kinds of prey for a mantis. _fly, bee, butterfly, grasshopper, caterpillar_
2. Does the prefix *fore-* in *forelegs* mean **four** or **front**? _front_
3. Are you likely to find a praying mantis hanging upside down at noon? _no_
4. How does the praying mantis get water? _It gets water from the insects it eats._

When it captures its prey, the mantis bites off and discards the head, eating the insect alive. Mantises are cannibals. After mating, the female mantis will often eat her mate simply because he is the nearest insect.

Day #4

1. The plural of *mantis* is _mantises_
2. Is a cannibal something that eats its prey alive or something that eats its own kind? _something that eats its own kind_
3. What is a good title for this paragraph? _What a Mantis Eat; Mantis Food_
4. What is your advice to a male mantis after mating: stay awhile or get out of there? _get out of there_

Name   **Week # 39**

Assessment

Echo-Echo!

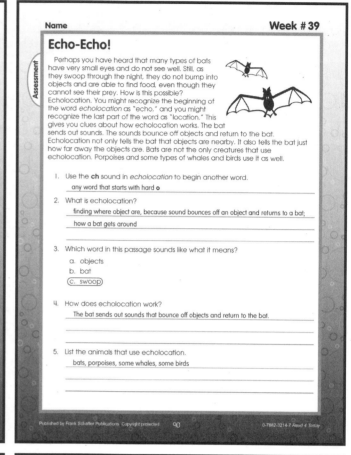

Perhaps you have heard that many types of bats have very small eyes and do not see well. Still, as they swoop through the night, they do not bump into objects and are able to find food, even though they cannot see their prey. How is this possible? Echolocation. You might recognize the beginning of the word *echolocation* as "echo," and you might recognize the last part of the word as "location." This gives you clues about how echolocation works. The bat sends out sounds. The sounds bounce off objects and return to the bat. Echolocation not only tells the bat that objects are nearby. It also tells the bat just how far away the objects are. Bats are not the only creatures that use echolocation. Porpoises and some types of whales and birds use it as well.

1. Use the *ch* sound in *echolocation* to begin another word.
   any word that starts with hard **o**
2. What is echolocation?
   finding where object are, because sound bounces off an object and returns to a bat;
   how a bat gets around
3. Which word in this passage sounds like what it means?
   a. objects
   b. bat
   c. swoop *(circled)*
4. How does echolocation work?
   The bat sends out sounds that bounce off objects and return to the bat.
5. List the animals that use echolocation.
   bats, porpoises, some whales, some birds

Name   **Week # 40**

Those Wacky Australian Animals
Australia's animals are unique. Australia has marsupials and monotremes. Marsupials are animals that carry their babies in pouches. A marsupial baby crawls into its mother's pouch and stays there until it is much bigger. Monotremes are mammals that give birth to their young by laying eggs, but they produce milk to feed their babies.

Day #1

1. What clues does the title give us about the subject of this article? _It is about animals in Australia that the author thinks are wacky._
2. What word in the title tells us the author has a sense of humor about the article? _wacky_
3. What is distinctive about monotremes? _They lay eggs but feed their babies with milk._
4. What is distinctive about marsupials? _The babies are carried in the mother's pouch._

The Tasmanian devil is a ferocious marsupial that lives on the island of Tasmania. These animals have black fur and very sharp teeth. They eat other mammals, birds, and reptiles.

Day #2

1. What kind of animal is the Tasmanian devil? _a marsupial_
2. What clues does the paragraph give you that is deserves the name *devil*? _It is ferocious and has sharp teeth._
3. How did the *Tasmanian* part of the animal's name come about? _It lives on the island of Tasmania._
4. Is the Tasmanian devil a carnivore? _yes_

The duck-billed platypus is one of two animals that hatches its young from eggs. It has soft fur, a snout, webbed feet and claws, and a flat tail like a beaver's tail. They live near rivers and creeks, where they eat crawfish, worms, and small fish.

Day #3

1. What kind of animal is the duck-billed platypus? _a monotreme_
2. What animal is compared with the duck-billed platypus in the paragraph? _beaver_
3. List the characteristics of the duck-billed platypus. List other animals that share one characteristic. You may want to make a chart. _soft fur, kitten; snout, pig; webbed feet, duck; claws alligator_
4. What do you think of the duck-billed platypus's looks? _Answers will vary._

Kangaroos are herbivores. Baby kangaroos, called joeys, live in their mother's pouch for 5 to 6 months. Kangaroos can hop at about 40 miles per hour (about 64.3 kph). They have strong hind legs for leaping about 30 to 40 feet (about 9 to 12 m).

Day #4

1. What does a herbivore eat?
   a. meat   b. plants *(circled)*   c. metal
2. What kind of animal is a kangaroo? _a marsupial_
3. How does a kangaroo get around? _by hopping_
4. Is the author right: Are Australian animals wacky? _Answers will vary._

Name   **Week # 40**

1. This title gives a lot of information. What does it tell us the author will do in this article?
   The author will compare Australia and the Untied States.

Assessment

Australia and the United States: Alike or Different?

How are Australia and the United States alike? How are they different? Australia is in the Southern Hemisphere. The United States is in the Northern Hemisphere. That means Australia's summer months are December through February, which are our winter months. Our summer months are June through August, which are their winter months. In the Northern Hemisphere, hurricanes and tornadoes spin in a clockwise direction. In the Southern Hemisphere they spin in a counterclockwise direction.

2. If you had a birthday on December 11, compare the activities you could do at your birthday party if you lived in Australia and if you lived in the United States.
   Answers will vary; perhaps a beach party in Australia and a skating party in the
   United States.

Australians drive on the left side of the road, while we drive on the right side of the road. Australia's population is about 19 million. That's about the same as the six most populated cities in the United States. Australia has kangaroos, anteaters, emus, and koalas, but here you'll find those animals only in zoos.

3. Do more people live in Australia or in the United States?
   the Untied States

The official head of Australia's government is the queen of England. Ours is the President. Australians elect people to a legislature, and a prime minister is the functional head of government. There are three major political parties there, but only two here. An Australian law says that people who are able to vote must vote. If not, they can be fined. There's no law like that in the United States.

4. Put the following topics in the order they appear in the article: population, politics, climate, wildlife, customs.
   climate, customs, population, wildlife, politics

5. What do you think is the most interesting difference between Australia and the United States?
   Answers will vary.
